W9-CCE-936

The Battle for
Wine and Love

The Battle for Wine and Love

OR

How I Saved the World from Parkerization

Alice Feiring

Harcourt, Inc.

Orlando Austin New York San Diego London

Copyright © 2008 by Alice Feiring

All rights reserved. No part of this publication may be reproduced
or transmitted in any form or by any means, electronic or mechanical,
including photocopy, recording, or any information storage and retrieval
system, without permission in writing from the publisher.

Requests for permission to make copies of any part of the work should be
submitted online at www.harcourt.com/contact or mailed to the following address:
Permissions Department, Houghton Mifflin Harcourt Publishing Company,
6277 Sea Harbor Drive, Orlando, Florida 32887-6777.

www.HarcourtBooks.com

Library of Congress Cataloging-in-Publication Data
Feiring, Alice.
The battle for wine and love: or how I saved the world
from parkerization/Alice Feiring.
p.   cm.
Includes index.
1. Wine and wine making.   2. Wine tasting.   I. Title.
TP548.F366   2008
641.2'2—dc22   2007034414
ISBN 978-0-15-101286-2

Text set in Bembo
Designed by Lydia D'moch

Printed in the United States of America
First edition
A C E G I K J H F D B

For my grandfather, Samuel Avrech,
one of the greatest loves of my life
and the very first winemaker I ever knew

– Contents –

The Battle for Wine and Love

– Introduction –

When it comes to wine and love, I get attached. So when I realized that certain wines I had relied on and lusted after were disappearing from the universe, I lost sleep. I angsted. I sulked. The loss was far more serious than the discontinuation of my favorite color of brick-red lipstick. Much more serious. In fact, the loss felt more like heartbreak. I could always find a different shade of lipstick, but there is no substitute for real wine or profound love.

I woke to this truth in 2001. The wine outlook was turning intensely bleak. Unless I navigated my choices very carefully, almost any wine would explode into a jammy fruit bomb, all vanilla–almond crunched up, often tampered with, and styled by technology and chemistry. This was not the kind of wine that first beguiled me. The revelation cattle-prodded my inner whistle blower. But the real eye-opener was a call from a California friend who told me, "You won't believe this, but there's a consultant out here who helps wineries beef up their wines so they'll score 90-plus Parker points" (referring to the world's most famous wine critic, Robert M. Parker, Jr.). He told me the name of the gentleman and company, Enologix, but said in true deep-throat style, "You didn't hear it from me."

I hadn't realized that the world of wine had become so cynical. A business was actually thriving by helping wineries shape and coerce a wine into a fat, oaky, thick, dense wine that Parker would give big points to? No wonder the Zinfandel I used to drink had lost its character and acquired as much alcohol as port. No wonder I could no longer find a California wine to suit me.

With all due apologies for painting Mr. Parker as the hit man in this book, he and his tastes have become bigger than himself. The term *Parkerized* has been added to the colloquial lexicon, and there is even a Wikipedia entry: *Wine Parkerization, the widespread stylization of wines to please the taste of influential wine critic Robert M. Parker, Jr.*

If Parker likes a wine, the wine sells. Prices rise. People make more money. Most everyone who equates high Parker points with increased income wants to please his palate.

One of the many disturbing outcomes of the rush to create a standardized wine is that it no longer matters where or on what you grow the grapes. Many Old World winemakers, with generations of winemaking in their history, believe that the grape is a vehicle for the land's expression. So the wine made in the Istrian Peninsula in Croatia will taste very different from the wine made in Lodi, California, even if the same grape is used. This quality—

alluring and seductive—drew me to wine in the first place and probably puts me firmly in a camp with others that Parker vilifies as "*terroir* jihadists" on his Web site, erobertparker.com. And those of us in that camp are mystified that the quest to attract Parker's attention has created wines with such concentrated power that delicacy and minerality are overpowered. And too often these wines rely on technology and additives to rack up Parker points.

So I dreamed: Wouldn't it be terrific if I could be the heroine who stems the tide, slows the overwhelming production of hormonally overblown or sanitized wines—the ones that the world's most famous wine critic is credited with championing? If only I could stop the proliferation of four-square wines with utterly no sense of place or minerality that reflect nothing about where they come from. At first I thought, *Write the screenplay:* Girl sleuth suspects a dangerous sameness in wine, discovers a link between the globalists gobbling up small wineries, technologies that change the nature of wine, and an influential critic. While investigating, she flies to a "safe zone," the Loire, and tastes wines so brilliant they bring tears to her eyes. She falls in love with a partisan vigneron, and together they create a network of like-minded individuals throughout the world, topple the critic's wine-rating system, put the conglomerates out of business, and return the vineyards of the world to those who know how to work them. In the end, our girl learns perfect French and lives happily ever after in love and in wine.

But at heart I'm a self-serving realist who sees how difficult it has become to grab a good glass at any price. With barbarians breaking down the door to the wine cellar, I had to shelve my fantasy and find the real story.

This is my journey into the wine world's version of David and Goliath. At stake is the soul of wine. This is giant corporation vs. independent winemaker. This is international and homogenous vs. local and varied. This is manipulated and technical wine vs. natural and artisanal. This is the world that courts Parker vs. those who heed their own calling. If the "new technology" made a better wine, I'd say great. But for the most part, wine is being reduced to the common denominator, and this is sacrilegious.

Throughout the journey, I visit producers who make wines that inspire love and devotion. I show how these wines are made. I unmask the modern way—the reverse osmosis, the tannin addition, the yeasts, the enzymes, the cold soaks, the sawdust, oak chips, the *barriques,* the micro- and macro-oxygenation, the rotor fermenters, and the cherry drops. There will be scientists and consultants, who help create cookie-cutter wines for the mass palate. I will deal with those who say *terroir* (the magic that brings soil, climate, vintage, and winemaker together in a bottle of wine) and natural wine making are simply excuses for bad wine.

I'm sure I won't change (nor do I wish to) the viewpoint of those perfectly happy to buy the wines that are easiest to find, but I am hoping to intrigue those who want wines that truly have a story to tell. Once people experience these wines and winemakers, once they know that wine truly does have soul and character, it will be difficult for them to cozy up to wines made by the numbers and not from the heart. I am not Cassandra predicting the fall of Troy, I am not Jonah warning Nineveh about impending destruction. I'm not even Samuel Beckett's Vladimir, wringing my hands in despair on the stage. There *is* hope. Though no jihadist, I am here to report that we are on the brink of a wine revolution, a renaissance. The best and most vibrant *real* wines are about to be born.

So, one day, I woke up to find that many wines I loved were disappearing. I went on a journey to find out why this was happening—who is behind this and what the hell does love have to do with it all.

– 1 –

The Age of Innocence

When my world was still innocent, I was drinking Manischewitz mixed with seltzer, but by the time my father ran off after a neighbor's wife, I was drinking the partially fizzy Mateus.

I had a multitude of reasons for disliking the object of Dad's affections, and all of them seemed to find expression in my developing a violent allergy to her Siamese cats and an aversion to her vulgar perfume. Obviously this Madame Chauchat of a woman had a profound effect on my sinuses. Nevertheless, I remain indebted to her. Years after my family's little scandal cooled down, Madame Chauchat and my father were cohabitating. I had run away to graduate school in the Boston area and was starting to cultivate an interest in wine. When I was visiting my father on a school break, his Madame Chauchat invited me to raid her ex-husband's wine cellar. Still terribly shy at twenty-three, I was

hesitant to appear greedy and so I took only three bottles out of the hundreds there. One was an Italian wine from Piedmont, a 1968 Barolo made by someone named Giovanni Scanavino. I packed the bottles carefully, took a nineteen-dollar People's Express flight back to Boston, and shared the wine with two friends and my boyfriend, a rather sweet but straightlaced guy who barely drank and who knew I didn't like that he barely drank. The drinking became an even bigger issue when he saw me take my first smell of the Barolo. As far as Mr. Straight Laced was concerned, it was as though I had just fallen in love with another man.

What was the attraction? Everything: the Barolo's aromas and tastes of rose petal and its suedelike tannin. There also was a bit of gravel and tar and tea. In later years I heard that most people couldn't understand this kind of "Old World–style" Barolo, a wine that in its youth was supposedly wildly rough, hard, and needed at least twenty years to reveal itself. In 1980, that Barolo was a preteen but it had already grown up gorgeous. I didn't need anyone to tell me it was phenomenal. I figured it out with my own nose.

As a pigtailed, freckled kid, I was obsessed with smells. My mother would nervously scold, "Stop smelling your food!" My father (a lawyer with a penchant for controversy) threatened to call the sheriff. My older brother mimicked me. They all finally threw up their hands, resigned to the fact that I was eccentric.

Waving everything under my nose before putting it into my mouth was as strong a reflex for me as sneezing. Sunkist orange-juice ice pop clutched in my little fist: Lick, sniff, lick. Friday night

dinner, Mom's fragrant tomato soup cupped in my spoon: Slurp, sniff, slurp. Nothing and no one could break me of this behavior.

They say that nontasters do not produce supertasters. In my case—with my mother and father being almost anosmiacs—the smell genes skipped a generation and landed in me. They came from my mother's father: Pop had a particularly prominent and fine nose. He must have seen that I was a kindred spirit because, when I was a wee one, he engaged me in early aroma training. He liked to keep little bottles of perfume in his long-underwear drawer, of all places. He would call to me, "Come, mameleh," wave scents under my nose, and then quiz me on what I perceived. He didn't speak much English and I had little Yiddish, but somehow we communicated just fine. When I was not much older, he would say, "Mameleh, a bissele schnapps?" and give me a fingernail amount of whiskey, but we always smelled it before we sipped. I'm grateful for learning how to enter the world nose first. My exaggerated sense of smell and taste are still my antennae to the world. They allow me to know what lobster and pigs' feet taste like (and to make appropriate wine pairings) though, having grown up in a kosher home, I have eaten neither. Smells have always warned me of danger, like the time I sniffed a trout from head to tail, refused to eat it, and was the only one at the meal who did not get sick. And romance would not be possible with a man who smells bad to me; conversely, it is an undeniable asset when a suitor smells like truffles.

My nose served me well when I landed north of Harvard Square in 1978. This was just before the world outside of New

York City discovered food, and I found myself longing for a crusty, dense loaf of bread and other delicacies I had taken for granted. But all was not lost. The upscale market Formaggio's Kitchen had opened down the street from my apartment. Needing employment while studying for a masters in dance/movement therapy, I worked behind the cheese counter and counseled the Brattle Street crowd on which goats were the most spectacular. When I found the Armenian section of town, where I could buy olives, stuffed grape leaves, pomegranate syrup, and ten kinds of feta, I was delighted. Boston was an ice-cream mecca, and my ability to blind taste through a dozen ice creams and identify all of them was my first claim to tasting supremacy. Friends encouraged me to go professional. Professional in what? I wondered. Working for an ice-cream company as a professional taster seemed a fast track to obesity. I don't think I could have handled the onslaught of aromas if I had become a perfumer's nose. The idea of leaving my chosen career in the psychotherapeutic use of movement for one in wine simply hadn't occurred to me yet.

A francophile roommate aided my transformation into a wine geek after my exposure to that Barolo. She and her gang gathered at our Depression-era triple-decker for weekly wine tastings, and I joined in. We systematically went through the wines of the world, many of them new to me. I wasn't interested in the details of winemaking at first. My modus operandi was to find out which wines I liked best and then greedily get to them before anyone else. We also drank a lot of wines coming out of California. It's funny to think that at one time I appreciated California Chardonnay, a wine I now rarely drink willingly. I also resonated with the rustic edge of Zinfandel. When the francophile moved out, my friend Honey-Sugar, a refugee from a starter marriage in Alabama, moved in. She and I expanded the wine tastings into monthly wine parties for eighteen, including the young wine collector who witnessed my first taste of Barolo.

Those with similar palates can pass significant chunks of time debating and discoursing on tasting minutiae. This sort of thing terribly bored the Young Collector's wife and my boyfriend, Mr. Straight Laced.

Yet, back then, I hadn't even picked up a wine book. I made an active decision to avoid studying. After all, wine study seemed too elitist for a child of the sixties. Even the thought of buying a proper, thin-lipped glass seemed snobby. I was positive that a paper cup or a ceramic mug would do. I let the Young Collector do the research. And being a bit of a horn-rim glasses kind of nerd, he was consumed by it. It was around this time, 1982 or so, when the Young Collector discovered someone named Robert M. Parker, Jr.

Parker had started his bimonthly newsletter, *The Baltimore-Washington Wine Advocate,* the very year that I moved to Boston. Inspired by the consumer advocacy of Ralph Nader and believing that most contemporary wine writers were "on the take," Parker saw himself offering a similar consumer service to wine lovers, based on impartiality and integrity. He doled out wine grades based on a 100-point system as if wines were biology exams. According to his unofficial biographer, Elin McCoy,

Parker started becoming what he is today just a year after he declared the 1982 Bordeaux vintage a slam dunk. Calling the vintage—when others did not—catapulted him to fame, and he was soon able to quit his job as a lawyer, devote himself to *The Wine Advocate,* and live life as a wine critic.

The Young Collector took Parker seriously for a number of years because he was seeking guidance and Parker was an "expert." The Young Collector wanted to build an age-worthy cellar, and there was no one else out there who was giving advice. Parker himself was green and didn't have the experience to know how wines aged, either. Nevertheless, when we decided to stage a Burgundy tasting, it was Parker's notes that guided us.

Now, it's all fine and good for me to bash Parker, but did I know anything more than he did? No. In fact, I didn't even know any Burgundy basics. I didn't even know what the grapes were—Chardonnay for white and Pinot Noir for red. I didn't know a grand cru (it sounded important) from a basic Bourgogne (which sounded less important). But I knew that Burgundy had a seductive mystique and was supposed to make me swoon.

The night of the Burgundy tasting, Mr. Straight Laced—who, by then, was trying hard to show me he could cozy up to wine, or at least take a few sips for love—remarked that one particular Burgundy smelled like a sweaty bicycle seat. Another smelled like pot to me (which, I now realize, isn't that unusual). Many wines not only tasted barn-yardy, which we were told was the mark of a true Burgundy, but even tasted like a barnful of cows and sheep and goats in the summer heat. By the time I was finished tasting the fifteen selections, my tongue and teeth were black from the tannic and bitter wine. Burgundy, seductive? I couldn't see anything in these wines but pain. I was embarrassed because I didn't like them. Was there something wrong with me? I wondered. I had always been so confident of my taste buds and nose. I didn't take consolation from the fact that the others in the room were also wondering what the big deal was with Burgundy. They just wanted something good to drink, so we pulled out the single-malt scotch.

Later, the Young Collector and I began to suspect that this new critic had a clay palate, especially since the one Burgundy we had both actually liked was a wine made by Guy Berthaut. Parker wrote about this baby in his 1990 book on Burgundy: "His 1983s tasted severe, terribly tannic, and dry, with traces of the ominous gout de sec. I just could not find enough fruit to balance out the tannins." The Young Collector had bought it as a challenge to Parker, who had rated it a lowly 75 points out of 100. We rated it terrific. The Young Collector then bought several bottles and laid them down. When we drank that wine fifteen years later, it had developed elegance and beauty. A great little wine.

AFTER A TEN-YEAR exile in Boston, I returned to New York at the end of August 1988 with only what I could fit into my beloved sixteen-year-old, rusted-out Toyota Corolla. The move must have been partly due to the fact that Mr. Straight Laced and I broke up in the rain while standing above the Seine on Pont Neuf. And Honey-Sugar had found her second husband, a

Parisian who wore ascots and thought the world was made up of two wines: Champagne and Bordeaux. It was time for change. I headed to New York to write fiction and while waiting for my big break, I would resign myself to life as a freelancer. I never did have a handle on the practical; my fiction could well be published posthumously, if ever, and New York needed another freelance writer the way the sea needs more salt. Somewhere around Hartford, I remember finding solace in the thought that I would fall in love again and this time the man would drink.

Even though I was a Brooklyn-born New Yorker, returning to the city was difficult. I felt too old for the housing I found, a three-hundred-dollar-a-month situation with a neurotic single-mother roommate that came with minor babysitting duties for the woman's fragile son. For this, I got the privilege of living in a closet on West 79th Street.

Not yet pressured by an abundance of paid deadlines, I used my downtime to taste. New York has a neverending stream of trade wine tastings. I finally had to overcome my shyness and take the initiative to network. I collected cards, called, and asked around. It worked. After attending just one tasting, I managed to wriggle into the scene and filled up my datebook with wine events. I attended them with as much fervor as I had New England contra dances. My very first was in the dark, wood-paneled room of Keens Steak House. A woman with porcelain skin and straw-blond hair handed me a list of one-hundred-plus Zinfandels to be tasted that day. Waiting to see what others do is unnatural for me; I am the type who invariably picks up the wrong fork for the fish course. Yet, I restrained myself, and when I saw suited-up men spitting into buckets I realized that the time for swallowing was over. With more than one hundred wines to be tasted, I'd have to follow their lead if I wanted to stay up on my heels. Now, this wasn't long after I'd learned which grapes were grown in Burgundy. I didn't know if I could manage the projectile force needed to send a beautiful arc of wine from mouth to bucket. Was the wine going to dribble out the corners of my mouth? What's more, I wondered, how do you taste a wine if you spit?

My first wine of the day was a Marietta Zinfandel from Geyserville, California. Back when I still counted Zinfandel as a lovely tipple, Marietta had been one of my favorites. I took a sip. The wine sat in my mouth getting warm as I pondered what to do with it. I remembered that Madame Chauchat's ex-husband (the one whose cellar I had raided) had taken wine-tasting classes. One morning at brunch, he had illustrated proper technique with a glass of grapefruit juice. He swirled the juice, then took some into his mouth, sort of gargled it, and then spit it out into another receptacle. I decided against the gargle but otherwise followed suit with the Marietta, spitting without embarrassing myself too badly.

My spit wasn't perfect, and I suffered from backsplash on my glasses. But I promised myself I'd get the hang of it, because I was determined to taste every wine on the table. It didn't take long to figure out that, by spitting, I could taste with greater precision. It was easier to break down the wine, analyzing weight, fruit, tannin, acid, and finish. I also realized that spitting doesn't mean that you don't take in alcohol. In time, I would develop a system: After every two wines, I would swirl and spit water to leach what I could from the inside of my cheeks.

Of that night, I remember little else except getting picked up by a salesman, who drove me back to 79th Street and tried to get his hands down my pantyhose. I was lonely in New York, but not that lonely. I scooted out from under his arm, thanked him for the ride, and ran up the fourteen flights of stairs.

By the following June, to my great relief, I found a real place to live. My flat on Elizabeth Street was a decent-sized walk-up with a leaky ceiling and a bathtub in the kitchen. Back then the neighborhood was still Little Italy. (Today it is called NoLita.) There were plenty of aging mafia soldiers on the block, and the old ladies stayed up summer nights playing cards and drinking coffee on the stoops and sidewalks until dawn. My friend Honey-Sugar took a job in New York, and commuted back to Boston and her French husband on weekends. In those days we often found ourselves at the bar at Union Square Café for a bowl of soup and bottomless glasses of wine provided by a generous bartender. Honey-Sugar, telling jokes in an even-stronger-than-usual Southern accent, was brilliant at getting us free refills. One night we tried out the nearby place Steak Frites. Honey-Sugar was in good form and the bartender, a stocky, goofy guy, suggested that when he got off work he should come over with Champagne. He turned out to be an actor, down on his luck and about to move back to his mom's home in New Jersey in defeat—Jim Gandolfini, later to be known as Tony Soprano. Jim showed up at our place, with two bottles of Dom Perignon, 1985. That Dom was my first. While Honey-Sugar and Jim were one-upping with the jokes, I tried to figure out what the big deal about this particular Champagne was. I was turning into a wine geek, like it or not.

WHILE TRYING TO develop my writer's chops, I landed work as a dance/movement therapist for the addicts of Gracie Square Hospital. The irony did not escape me. I felt pangs of guilt wondering why I could drink and they could not. When I got my first real wine story, a feature on Long Island wine for *Connoisseur* magazine, I kept the topic of the article secret from my mental-health colleagues, most of whom were in recovery.

I can't say I was a big fan of Long Island wines in 1990 (to me, they tasted like potatoes and cabbage), but I was thrilled with the assignment. I was also nervous. I felt I had to hide my inexperience. I pretended to be an old hand at tasting wines from barrels in the frigid cold at eight in the morning. I pretended that it wasn't the first time I spat on the floor instead of into a bucket. I pretended I had the knowledge to assess the wine. I may not have had the knowledge—I didn't even know how wine was made—but I did have the instinct and the palate and enough writing ability to put together a one-thousand-word story on the evolution of a new wine region.

At the end of the day I was invited to dinner with the premier couple of the Long Island wine scene. While she put the finishing touches on her salmon, he escorted me upstairs to see his original passion, rare books. When he made a pass at me, I pretended not to understand and hurried downstairs to play with their dog and gab to my hostess about how she and her husband came to plant grapevines on Long Island instead of potatoes. Somewhere in the middle of a very uncomfortable meal, her husband remarked how much I looked like Woody Allen, and asked if I was by any chance Jewish. I later found out that the winemaker told my editor, "That girl knew nothing about wine." There goes the wine-writing career, I thought.

But the cad winemaker was almost right. I knew almost nothing about wine, and I had a long way to go. Feeling too poor to take a proper wine-tasting class, I continued tasting like mad, finally bought my first wine books, decided thin-lipped wineglasses were far superior to paper cups and jelly glasses, and voraciously learned with every drop.

I was most interested in the opportunity to find out more about my first wine love, Barolo. But Barolos were so expensive; the opportunity to drink them didn't come often. Luckily, I had made a new friend who shared with me wines that I had only read about or tasted in parsimonious pours at trade events. This man, a violin-bow maker, had become an early Parker points addict. (Eventually, buying up as many highly rated Parker wines as he could, he went into bankruptcy.) While he was still solvent, a few of us were frequent visitors to his tiny Upper West Side apartment. He would fold his Murphy bed into the wall, and we'd set to work eating cheese and drinking the new, super-duper Parker stars, such as Parusso and Scavino. After tasting these Barolos, I was as befuddled as I had been at the Cambridge Burgundy tasting. I didn't get it. Of course the wines were young, but they were supposedly made in the "modern" style in order to make the wine easier to drink young! Yet to me they were hard. They were flat. They were chewy. They had as much subtlety as a Louis XIV chandelier. They were a far cry from my beloved 1968 Giovanni Scanavino. I called the Young Collector in Boston and warned him not to buy any of these newfangled Barolos. But it was too late. He had already taken Parker's recommendations and passed up some old-fashioned, classic Barolos for these newbies. That was the last year the Young Collector fell for Parker's advice. And even though the generous bow maker had lots of plusses, I was sure I could never be smitten with a man who loved these soulless wines.

How did I grow into a woman who has a hard time accepting heroes, even wine heroes? Maybe it had something to do with my father's leaving home in such a brutal way. Maybe it goes back to marching against the Vietnam War or being brought up with my nose pressed to the glass of the sexual and political revolutions of the sixties. Whatever the reason, I was immune to the opinions of Robert Parker, the voice that was guiding a nation of passionate wine lovers.

The whole Parker force passed me by for quite some time. I noticed him, I noticed our differences, but I didn't take him too seriously. I was not at all interested in his points. Instinctively, I never went in for scores. The idea of buying a wine—so sensitive a product—because it had 98 Parker points seemed silly, like going into a profession because the numbers on an aptitude test say you should.

MY SELF-EDUCATION was leading to bylines in magazines like *Condé Nast Traveler* and the *New York Times,* but I was still living just above poverty level. I thought hard: What else could I do?

While writing a story on the wines of the Bandol region of Provence for next to nothing for *The Wine News,* I called up Victor of V.O.S. Wines of Excellence, who imported a particular Bandol I wanted to try. Victor told me he knew I'd never make any money for my retirement by writing about wine, so why didn't I grow up and sell wine for him?

I took him up on the offer. Turns out, I was a miserable salesperson. No Dale Carnegie. I could not master the art of the deal. My clients liked me, and they loved the wines I shared with them. But they bought from other people, real salespeople. My poor sales record didn't bother Victor, though. For some reason, he liked having me around—fortunately for me. Working at Victor's kept me from writerly isolation, gave me the inside scoop on some great wine stories, and accelerated my learning.

Victor had a very Old World, anti-Parker palate. He loved high acidity and subtle fruit, and mocked the wines coming in that reeked of vanilla and toast. He introduced me to a few Burgundies so wonderful they made me whistle in appreciation. Many of these were wines that would give Parker hives, because they were on the leaner side, with fruit under the surface rather than out there punching you in the face. They were made mostly in old dingy cellars whose walls were covered in thick mold—an environment Parker felt was unsanitary and bad for wines. I loved the wines from the *negoçiant* Camille Giroud, a very old-fashioned, eccentric house. When I had their 1969 Nuits St. George, I thought it tasted like peonies pressed between the pages of a treasured novel. (In 2002, Camille Giroud was bought by the California wine auctioneer Anne Colgin, who also lends her name to a California cult Cabernet, and a group of investors. The wine has since lost some of its Old World rusticity.)

Meanwhile, despite Victor's insistence that wine sales was a better living than wine writing, and even though I knew plenty of salespeople with six-figure incomes, my bank account was not growing nearly as much as my wine education. When I was approached by the editors of *Food & Wine* to take on the mammoth and lucrative job of writing the magazine's official wine guide, I knew it was an offer I couldn't refuse. I was charged with finding hundreds of wines to recommend, and in the name of research tasting huge numbers of wines from around the world. *How better to learn?* I thought. Perhaps I would even find other wines with the magic of that Barolo. The adventure was going to be quite a ride.

The night I signed the contract, I shared a bottle of Champagne with the man I was in love with, the Owl Man. While he was often extremely difficult, he also had the highly developed olfactory skills of a bat. He reminded me so much of my grandfather, and we shared a love of wine. I had been saving this particular

Champagne from my Boston days. Inhaling its aroma, we both gave thanks that I had found a profession where smelling before drinking or eating was—unquestionably—socially acceptable.

I broke the news to Victor that I could no longer sell for him. I couldn't risk the appearance of conflict of interest over the paltry two grand I made from being a slacker salesperson. He protested that British writers sell and write about wine all the time. That might be true, I said, but I couldn't take the chance. Then Victor blessed me. "May you be the world's next Robert Parker—except knowledgeable and discerning enough that you can help me stop selling wine by the points."

SOON ENOUGH, I was midbook and desperate. For starters, I was overwhelmed by the menacing mountains of bottles that needed tasting. And thanks to the winning combination of uncorking and intense typing, I developed carpal tunnel syndrome. Most significantly, while spitting the contents of countless bottles into my stainless-steel sink, I concluded that almost every wine tasted too damned alike. Clunky, foursquare wines, all! What had happened to the wine universe? Though I may have been ignoring Robert Parker, obviously other wine writers, makers, and buyers were not. Wine publications—including the very influential *Wine Spectator*—had long since adopted the Parker model of the 100-point scoring system. The world was seeking any wine with a 90+ to bring home for dinner.

Elin McCoy writes in her 2005 book, *The Emperor of Wine: The Rise of Robert M. Parker, Jr., and the Reign of American Taste,* that around the millennium (when I was writing the *Food & Wine* book), Parker was at the height of his power. In her "Scoring Parker" chapter, she says that in the 1980s he cemented his reputation and ushered in a kind of criticism that "woke up winemakers everywhere." By the 1990s his influence was worldwide: he had created the new market for fine wine and brought financial gain to many wine growers. "Now, in the first decade of the twenty-first century," she concludes, "he found himself an American icon, which meant, of course, that he had become a brand name." The wines that stacked up at my door and dribbled into my glass were testaments to his brand. I had to reckon with the Parker power if I were to understand why most of what I tasted was the rough vinous equivalent of Hawaiian Punch.

As growers tried to capture Parker's attention, the spectrum of wines' tastes narrowed. Wines were becoming standardized, or as Jonathan Nossiter points out in his film documentary *Mondovino,* globalized. These "styled" wines were everywhere. A good name for them would be "Everyman," as they had no distinguishing qualities, no sense of place. White or red, they were big, oaky fruit bombs with gobs of jam. It seemed like, in a flash, wines from the Old World (such as Greece, Spain, and Italy) started to taste like those of the New World—that is, the younger wine regions (such as Australia, Chile, and California).

I loved wines with a sense of place. But place disappeared. I liked wines with an edge. Edge disappeared. I liked wines with earth in them. Earth disappeared. And what took their place? Boring fruit, fruit, fruit and oak, oak, oak. The kinds of wines I drank were disappearing like wild horses into the sunset. I loved Rioja. There were still a *few* wines left that tasted like Rioja but (I suspected) not for long. Italy? I used to love Tuscan wines, but they all tasted like California wines now. And poor Piedmont, the birthplace of my Barolo—the area had been devastated by the invasion of those New World, toasty flavors, which leave espresso breath and a splintery taste in their wake. And, I wondered, what the hell was strawberry-vanilla jam—like some Body Shop concoction—doing in my Nuits St. George?

The chief culprit, I suspected, was winemakers' love affair with aging entire vintages in brand-new, small, very expensive, highly toasted barrels called *barriques*. The result of this technique was often a terrible sameness, the wines all overpowered with aromas and flavors like cherry vanilla, toast, cookie dough, espresso, and butter. I am no winemaker, but I wondered: Didn't they know that those barrels could also make wine extremely bitter?

Another trendy technique was to extend the grapes' hang time. I have always believed that the beginning of the end for many wines I once worshipped came with a 1993 California Zinfandel and a love poem Parker composed to its maker, Helen Turley. Turley's Hayne Vineyard Zinfandel broke the charts with a gushy 95 points from both Parker and the other major global wine authority, the *Wine Spectator*. It was the highest-scoring Zinfandel up until that time. Parker rhapsodized: "Frankly, Zinfandel does not get much richer than this. The texture is akin to syrup, with a thickness and richness that must be tasted to be believed." While this style might be perfect for people who love a thick, syrupy-sweet cola, it doesn't work for me. I was always crazy about seltzer with a spritz of fresh lime or lemon.

Helen Turley left the grapes on the vines as long as she possibly could to squeeze as much fruit as possible out of them. And, hoping to win high scores for their wines, more and more growers went with a long hang time. Some people—like me—think this method creates overripe, "stupid" wines, with no structure or longevity. The trend has also given rise, in the New World especially, to a propensity for highly alcoholic wines. Some people say it's global warming that has raised alcohol content from an average of 12.5 to 14.5 percent—with some levels as high as 17 percent (port is 20 percent)—but extended hang time is more like it.

When Parker rewarded this style and anointed Turley the high priestess of wines, California growers rushed to imitate her big, jammy style in all their wines. Shortly afterward, the rest of the world followed and the dumbing down of wine commenced.

I saw wines that were delicate by nature receive low scores. I overheard people in restaurants complain of a wine being "thin." People trying to learn about wine had swallowed the myth that a good wine is a thick wine. Rumors spread that corporate owners handed out bonuses to winemakers who produced high scorers. The paradigm of a great wine shifted to one big, jammy, oaky fruit bomb, and the whole industry adjusted accordingly. This led to situations like one in December 2006, when Wither Hills, a New Zealand winery, was accused of doctoring its Sauvignon Blanc to make it bigger and fruitier to get a higher score in a competition.

Welcome to Big Wine. When a wine got a 94+ score, bottle prices climbed, the wine sold out, and money was made all around. Wine was traded on the NASDAQ; wines became "brands"; big brands gobbled up little ones. The style of wine I craved—authentic, reflective of its climate and soil—began to disappear.

Though I had watched the wine business grow, obviously I'd been sheltered from the results until I worked on the *Food & Wine* book. Now I saw clearly that wines—red or white—were virtually all fruit, vanilla, and toast, the vinous equivalent of bottle blonds. I was utterly miserable. *The book I'm writing,* I thought, *is going to be very short.*

There *were* a few bright spots. A few importers were scouting out some of Europe's best. Most notably, I started to trust those imports from Kermit Lynch, New York's Neal Rosenthal and Becky Wasserman, who was based in Burgundy. But at one point I realized that the greatest number of the wines I enjoyed had the back label of Louis/Dressner. I found that those wines conveyed a time and place so pure and complex that they tasted revolutionary. So I did what most wine writers do. I called to ask for samples.

A strong Queens-accented voice answered the phone. "Louis Dressner."

"Joe, please?" I asked.

"This is Louis," the voice retorted.

Through my industry connections I'd learned that there was no Louis as he said it, enunciating the *s* at the end. Louis—pronounced Lou-wee—was the last name of Joe Dressner's wife.

I persisted, and in a few minutes he backed down, turned shockingly good-natured, and eventually concluded I wasn't some predatory wine writer looking for freebies to serve at my next dinner party. "Come over tomorrow," he offered. "I'll have a lot open."

Joe Dressner's office, on the edge of Little Italy and Soho, was a five-minute bike ride from my home. He opened the door for me, sucking on a cigarette. In all ways, he was a looming presence. His feet (the size of skateboards) could have squished me like a roach. He shared the narrow office with his wife, Denyse; their dog, Buster; their partner Kevin; several hundred wines; and Joe's bicycle.

I went to work tasting the wines. At first, like a cat, Joe ignored me. Then like a dog, he warmed up, getting positively verbose. He told me that he, an ex-Marxist, ex–radical activist (of course, I was impressed) had met his French wife at NYU's school of journalism. Wanting to find something that would give them a cross-Atlantic livelihood and a way to live half of the year in France, they got into the wine-import business. He used to import conventional stuff, anything he thought had a market, and thought it was immaterial how the wines were made. He slowly came to the conclusion that what he called "real" wines tasted better than the conventional ones—and he also found the winemakers more simpatico. He started to get rid of wines he called "spoofulated," those that were manipulated for flavor.

I spent hours at Joe's, getting the dirt on his life as well as the wines, like a white Burgundy that did not finish its fermentation for nearly two years—something, he said, that a New World winemaker would never allow or have the patience for. Most modern wine folk like fast ferments—a week, maybe two weeks at most. Big Joe kept dropping intriguing terms: *native yeast, naturally made, organic, old barrels, biodynamics.* While I got most of the lingo, I didn't let on that I didn't have a clue what a "natural wine" was, or that I knew next to nothing about biodynamics (though I had an inkling it was some kind of homeopathic approach to farming). I had heard that a cool cosmetic company, Dr. Hauschka, used biodynamically grown botanicals, and something about the teetotaling founder of the Waldorf Schools, philosopher Rudolph Steiner, who had also founded biodynamics and died in the 1920s. But several of the wines I'd already earmarked as winners turned out to be made either purely or in part with biodynamics. When I tasted a Côt (the name for Malbec in the Loire) from Clos Roche Blanche—a winery that was flirting with biodynamics at the time—my palate zinged. The wine tasted like velvety violet petals sucked through a chalk straw. Seeing my pleasure, Joe told me about the two-person operation that made the wine. At twenty-one, upon her father's death, Catherine Roussel took over the family winery. Didier, a man who showed up to pick grapes in 1978, became partner and the winemaker who made that Côt from one-hundred-year-old gnarled vines in a field composed mostly of yellow limestone (*tuffeau*) soil in the Loire. *Note to self: Must visit there one day and see what the soil looks like and meet the people who make this gorgeous wine.*

Now that Big Joe and I were so chummy, I expressed my dissatisfaction with the bulk of the wines I was tasting for my project.

"The problem is bigger than oak," Joe said. "Yeasts. It's the yeasts." He enunciated the word emphatically, as if echoing the word *plastics* in *The Graduate*.

I was never a crack science student, but to understand the yeast issue I had to tackle fermentation. Putting it into a wine context, helpfully, made chemistry easier for me to fathom.

It turns out that if grapes are healthy, and from healthy, alive soil, they have a hefty yeast population clutching their skin, so that fermentation should start spontaneously during or shortly after the grape crush. These yeasts gobble fruit sugars, transforming them into alcohol, expelling CO_2 along the way. When there's nothing else for them to eat, the yeasts keel over, die, and alcoholic fermentation is done. There are several variants of yeast—Saccharomyces—that live both on the grape and in wineries. All of them help in the transformative process of fermentation. Only one yeast, however, can stand up to the heat produced during fermentation and finish the job. This muscle man of a yeast is known as the wine yeast: *Saccharomyces cerevisiae*. If this yeast is not present in great enough numbers, the winemaker is in trouble. Take my grandfather's story.

My grandfather was the first winemaker I ever knew. A White Russian born the year the lightbulb was invented, 1888, he arrived in America in 1919 and by the time of Prohibition was vinifying in the basement. Every year, Pop would spend a lot of money on grapes and equipment. Ninety percent of the time, he ended up with vinegar instead of wine. He couldn't figure out what he was doing wrong. As an Orthodox Jew he probably got his winemaking ideas from the Book of Genesis. He bought the grapes at the market and then, like Noah, crushed them and waited. He didn't use sulfur, which came into use with the Phoenicians to kill off organisms and bugs that can cause trouble. If Pop were alive today I could give him my diagnosis. His grapes didn't have enough of the good yeast. His basement, filled with petrochemical fumes from the oil burner, didn't have a healthy yeast population. His unsulfured wine didn't have a chance. He had an acetobacteria problem.

Pop found out that making wine with such little intervention carries emotional and financial risk—risks that many modern winemakers don't want to take. Interesting to note, however, young, Old World winemakers who learned how to handle the natural process from parents or grandparents don't feel this threat. Plenty of winemakers around the world have never lost a vintage because they know how to work naturally, because the knowledge was passed down from their elders. They also know that natural yeast is a part of the *terroir*, that it carries the DNA of the vintage, the dirt, the climate, the vines, the grape, and the cellar, and that no wine can tell a story without it.

Big Joe said that the best, most historic example of the transformational power of industrial yeast was that of Georges Duboeuf, the wine giant who made Beaujolais Nouveau a household name. (Leading most people to forget that Beaujolais, the real stuff, was a yummy wine to take seriously.) In the 1980s, by using the yeast 71B (to be precise), Georges Duboeuf changed the nature of Beaujolais. Instead of its characteristic aromas and flavors of ground ivy mixed with wild strawberries, the wine was reinvented with banana overtones. In fact, many wine critics started to seek banana as a sign of authenticity in a Beaujolais.

In today's globalized wine scene, winemakers would like to make wine as standardized as possible. Adding industrial yeast to the wine helps. It ensures that fermentation will start and finish when the winemaker wants it to, not according to the whims of nature. This is extremely important when Costco is expecting its new shipment of wine from Gallo in April—plus, the retailer doesn't want the customer to bring the wine back complaining that it doesn't taste like last year's model.

Louis Pasteur helped winemakers achieve greater control when he identified yeast as integral to fermentation, and his discovery led to the manufacture of industrial replicas. Before the mid-1970s, yeasts came in only two flavors: one for red wine and one for white. Initially, they were not promoted for their flavor- or aroma-altering ability, but used to ensure that the job of fermentation got done. Now, instead of only two yeast possibilities, the market offers about 150 different, finely tuned designer yeasts to give wine whatever flavor characteristics the winemaker wants.

In some instances, using a nonaromatic industrial yeast makes sense, even to a purist like me. Since native yeast reflects the characteristics of the land, if the land is farmed with chemicals or is more suited for cabbage than grapes—as I believe is true of Long

Island—yeast from the packet might be a whole lot safer and might make the wine taste a lot better. But the situation has gotten completely out of hand. Many wineries are proud of their industrial yeasts. Press releases from Hogue in Washington State have described their yeast selections, such as Y3079 and D254. One just in from E & J Gallo, its Bridlewood brand label boldy touts, *Designer yeast!* The wine world has gone topsy-turvy.

That yeast conversation in Big Joe's little office clarified so much for me. The reason my neutral-smelling Albarinos had started to sometimes smell like the cat pee of Sauvignon Blanc was because winemakers dumped in designer yeast to change the texture, aroma, and flavor of the wines. What do you want? Mangos? Strawberries? Cocoa? Cherry? Winemakers could now go to the yeast selection the way perfumers could go to the flavor and fragrance suitcase.

Until then, I had trusted that wine was made in the vineyard, from soil and grapes. Now I realized that most wine was highly manipulated in the winery. And, it turns out, the problem is even bigger than yeast. Today's winemakers can manipulate their wines in all sorts of new and frightful ways to make them more Parker pleasing as well as easier to micromanage.

Now, a new genetically modified yeast strain, called ML01, has been commercialized and is authorized for use in the United States. It promises to produce a cleaner, faster fermentation and, in the future, could catch a hangover before it begins. Another additive, yeast food (urea), keeps fermentation going even when the grapes are extraripe and the sugars quite high. Bacteria is often added to start malolactic fermentation—the fermentation that usually follows alcoholic fermentation and softens the malic acid (think green apple) to lactic acid (think milk). Enzymes are used to build color and modify flavor. Mega Purple, a grape additive, boosts color and "mouthfeel." Wood tannins build texture, and finishing agents like gelatin also aid good mouthfeel and remove bitterness. There are also chemical defoaming and microbial-control agents. Velcorin is a popular microbial. According to the Scott Lab Web site, it is "moderately toxic by ingestion, highly toxic by inhalation, irritating to the skin and eyes and combustible if exposed to an open flame. Due to these hazards, people are required to wear safety gear when handling Velcorin and are given regular safety training."

In the vineyards, irrigation not only keeps vines hydrated no matter how dry the season, but is also used to assist in the super-ripening of the grapes, which has been in fashion ever since the mid-1990s. I believe that grapes lose their individuality and ability to translate *terroir* when they reach very high sugar content. Trying to ferment grapes with such high sugars can also make a lot of trouble in the winery—trouble that calls for a high-tech fix.

Machines are now used to change the nature of wine. Two of them are peddled by Vinovation, a California company owned by Clark Smith. For those who want a smoothie instead of a wine, micro-oxygenation is the ticket. The micro-ox bubbler erases tannins that come from the seeds, stems, and skins of a grape. I don't know why tannin, a natural and essential by-product of grapes, became a dirty word. I find that it keeps ripe fruit from turning into a cloying wine. Tannin also gives wine its bones. With time, rough tannins develop and evolve and give wine great complexity. In a world that doesn't want to wait a few years for a wine to age up, this machine helps to make wine smooth immediately. I suppose that if micro-oxygenation helped make an amazing wine, I couldn't argue. But to me, it turns wine into baby food, stripping it of texture and complexity. A wine emasculated of tannins is robbed of a dignified and multilayered old age.

Jason Lett, a fervent young winemaker in Oregon, son to one of the state's founding winemakers, David Lett, is trying to do right by wine. He told me, "The machine is purported to do in weeks what takes months or years in a barrel. The salesmen even claim that you can make wine without barrels. Make your wine in a tank, throw in those oak planks or tea bags of oak dust or chips [commonly used in inexpensive wine] for that vanilla flavor the U.S. market so adores. Tanks are far more economical than barrels, and so the bean counters are pushing this approach."

The use of these techniques is not limited to high-production commercial wines. Many wines passed off as "artisanal" use any number of these processes as well. Paradoxically, as with many of these newfangled techniques—including industrial yeasts—the birthplace of micro-oxygenation was France. The winemaker Patrick Ducournau developed *microbullage,* in the States called micro-oxygenation (and often shortened to micro-ox), in Madiran to help tame the wildly tannic grape Tannat. Proponents of micro-oxygenation argue that the process is low-tech—essentially, a slender wire pulses bubbles of oxygen into the barrel. Clark

Smith likens it to whipping egg whites for a soufflé. Still, I see it as such a texture and flavor changer that it's like a microwave for wine. Little is worse in my view.

At one time during my long and intricate relationship with the Owl Man, he insisted we have a microwave. The dark box sat on top of the refrigerator, staring menacingly at me. I undertook a blind-tasting campaign to prove my point that the contraption ruins food. When the Owl Man tasted a microwaved potato alongside one that was properly baked, he definitely tasted the difference. But when he tasted the difference between micro-waved milk and milk heated up on the stove, he threw the ma-chine out.

Another of Clark Smith's machines performs reverse osmosis, which he likes to call ultrafiltration. This machine is a torture chamber that deconstructs the wine into water, alcohol, and sludge. The machine can also concentrate wine, reduce alcohol, restart a stopped fermentation (a problem with those high-sugar grapes), and eliminate mold. (Yikes! What are today's winemakers doing to end up with a mold problem?) But its main purpose in America is to de-alcoholize wine to achieve balance and save money. (Wine that is over 14 percent alcohol is taxed at fifty cents a gallon.) The device allows a winemaker to envision the flavor, texture, and alcohol, then turn the knob to create the wine to specs. Smith likens this to finding a wine's "sweet spot." The reverse-osmosis machine is to wine what digital technology is to film and music. It removes the depth, a loss that seems to paral-lel other trends in today's mass culture.

Winemakers these days are getting more comfortable admitting their use of micro-ox. But reverse osmosis and additives? Clark Smith proudly states their use on his own labels, but most winemakers are not so forthcoming. Finding out if a winemaker is using these is as hard as getting information from the Department of Homeland Security. Obviously, winemakers don't want to add a list of ingredients to their label. They aren't legally required to, either. They are rightfully fearful of advertising the reverse-osmosis process, believing that the public would "misunderstand."

Often the proponents of high-tech argue that without technology we'll return to a Dark Age where wine, like my grandfather's, will mostly turn to vinegar. They shake their fingers accusingly, saying that you can't stop progress. I find this kind of technological "progress" similar to the modernization of foods in the 1950s, when frozen was lionized as better than fresh. What followed was twenty-five years of the Dark Ages for food. I'm not sure that was progress. Technology might make a serviceable tomato, but can anything improve on or replace the lusciousness of a juicy, succulent tomato grown the old-fashioned way?

I wrote about Clark Smith and the high-tech wine world. Clark was a sport about it. But we were clearly on opposite sides of the argument, so I was surprised when, on a visit to New York, he suggested lunch.

I met Clark and his wife, Susie, at Manhattan's Osteria Del Circo. At some point in the meal, I returned from a toilet run to find three glasses of white wine standing in front of my place setting. "Tell me which one you like better," Clark said.

Blind tasting is the only way to really tune in to a wine. The Owl Man came into our relationship a believer in the wine Mouton-Cadet, perhaps the Yellow Tail of its time. Only when I made him taste it against other wines did he realize how bad it was. But blind tasting can also be terrifying, especially when you're put on the spot. Obviously I was being set up, but for what?

The first Chardonnay had cleaner flavors; it was in fact a little squeakier. The second felt hotter in my mouth, much hotter. In fact, there was some overripe fruit, but it told me something about where the wine came from. The third was just very wacked out, all over the place, the balance of fruit, alcohol, and acid was so off that it almost didn't seem like wine. Beauty is in the details. I like wines that grab me with irregularity. My mother once told me that my old roommate Honey-Sugar would be so beautiful "if she only had a nose job." The truth is, my friend is beautiful period. The truth was that I liked none of the three wines, but the second one was the most interesting. I said so. Clark's wife's neck so tensed up that her pearls started to jiggle. Clark's lips thinned out. "How can you possibly like that one better?" he asked. Susie started to sputter.

It turns out that the three wines started out life as the same, high-alcohol wine. One Chardonnay was in its natural state at 15.3 percent alcohol. The other two had been treated with reverse osmosis. One had been taken down to about 12 percent and another to the "sweet spot," in the 12.9 percent range. The one I chose hadn't been messed with. Clark and Susie were appalled. It was too much. I didn't eat oysters, I didn't eat prosciutto, and I didn't like their processed wine. What would I do next?

Some years after that experience, Clark is nice enough to let bygones be bygones. He thinks that we both want the same things: natural, *terroir*-driven wines. He views himself as a proponent of naturally made, expressive wines, and all of the machines he promotes as tools to help wines achieve this. He gave me the update on his business's health:

At present, we have about eight hundred California customers and four hundred in the rest of the U.S. and overseas. Between us and the Spinning Cone [the other technology that reduces alcohol content], we now adjust alcohol on about 45 percent of the premium wine California produces.

You're right that a sea change has occurred in the way we're viewed. Stories like the ones you've written have focused attention on the issues winemakers face, and while at first horrified, journalists have indeed become more understanding.

I am still horrified. I am less horrified if winemakers fess up to the processing and tinkering. I support campaigns for transparency. A wine label should list all additives and processes used. If you fake oak flavor with chips or dust, put it on the label. Yeast and enzymes? Yup. Chestnut tannin? Of course. What about the use of flavor, texture, and alcohol-adjustment machines? You bet. How many New World winemakers would be able to put something as simple as *Wine made from grapes* on their labels? Fewer and fewer all the time.

It's a fun sport for me to try out those country wine stores with neon Budweiser signs in the windows to see if they have anything in stock that I could possibly drink in a wine emergency. Most of their selections turn out to be brands owned by the wine giants Gallo and Bronco, which to me means wines made by the numbers. But there is usually something from the Rhône for sale, and that's my standby safe choice. But I don't have to go to the wilds of the Catskills to find a shop filled with bad wine. I don't have to go farther than the store across the street. I'm an urbanite, and I live on a block that has become impossibly hip. The store crew think they make an effort. They do make an effort; they just don't know how to succeed.

As I explored this New World wine vs. Old World dichotomy, another theme kept coming up: confusion surrounding the word *tradition*. There were so many meanings, applied to different ends. Some people, like Clark, used it as a weapon, as a synonym for poorly made wine, for wine that turned into vinegar.

But what did traditional winemaking mean to me? I wasn't sure.

I needed to find a new way to describe wines that I liked. Perhaps I was using the word *traditional* when I meant *authentic*.

The man to have this conversation with, I realized, was my mentor, Big Joe. I hadn't seen Big Joe for a while, so I invited him out to tea at Podunk, a stern little tea shop on East Fifth Street. I told him about my struggles to define traditional wine.

Big Joe gave me a solid lecture about how using the word *tradition* in the wine world was dangerous.

"Remember," he said, "there used to be a lot of bad wine made, and a lot of that could be called 'traditional.' Traditional could mean chemical farming—because for a time, that was the convention. Traditional could mean adding acidity to a wine, because that was the common practice."

"I see," I said. "Within these parameters, fast food could be the traditional cuisine of America."

"Exactly."

"So what do you mean by traditional? Brooks Brothers? Classic?"

"Authentic," he said.

The very word I had been thinking of. We were in agreement. The more I thought about it, the dogma of authentic wines would include

Healthy farming practices
Hand picking
No extended cold maceration
No added yeasts or bacteria
No added enzymes
No flavors from oak or toast
No additives that shape flavor or texture
No processes that use machines to alter alcohol level, flavor,
   or texture or that promote premature aging

Was that too much to ask? Was I asking for something as impossible as emptying a lake with a slotted spoon or fetching black water from the River Styx? Perhaps so. But before I gave up on the situation, I had to get on a few planes.

– 2 –

What I Learned at UC Davis

Back in the old, carefree days, I found myself in a state of near-undress with a man I found adorable. He rode a motorcycle, sang medieval music, had a jester's costume, and danced in the street when he wasn't at his more manicured job as a computer geek. Shortly into our session he barked out a list of instructions: "To the left. Up. Harder. To the right. There. Turn forty-six degrees. Softer. Back up. No, you don't have it."

I felt that I was engaged in a driver's education class instead of foreplay. All of the sudden I wasn't in the mood.

I recalled this episode often during my conversations with Clark and other winemakers who were obsessed with control. I certainly thought about it again when I visited a town and wine region on the central coast of California called Paso Robles. This is an up-and-coming wine region located halfway between Los Angeles and San Francisco. While known for ancient Zinfandel vines, it has made a name for itself in the Rhône grape varietals, especially Syrah.

When I arrived in town, it was buzzing with the excitement of a recent visit by Robert M. Parker, Jr. Word on the street was that Parker went home a Paso fan. I was curious to see what the critic liked. In the rising heat of late afternoon, I stepped out of my rental and into the Robert Hall Winery car park, hot enough to sear a tuna. Eager to get inside to my air-conditioned appointment, I still had my misgivings. Through a quick Internet search I had learned there was a real man named Robert Hall, who had "retired" to winemaking after a career in real-estate development that had been jump-started with the building of several bowling centers. His new winery was a state-of-the-art affair, with over nineteen thousand square feet of recently fabricated underground caves. According to the Hall Web site, the winery's goal in crafting its wine was to capture the exceptional color and flavor that is the essence of Paso Robles.

The winery write-up posted on the Paso Robles Wine Country Alliance Web site alerted me that this was probably not an Alice Feiring–approved winery. I learned that the winemaker, Texan-born-and-educated Donald Brady helped to put Texas wine on the map. Brady had also worked at the megacommercial Delicata wine operation, was spoken of as a respected member of the wine community, and had received the International Wine and Spirits Competition Wine of America Award. The Web site said his goal was to "capture the essence of the vineyard as well as enhance the quality of wine by getting the best product possible out of each vine."

Robert Parker, meanwhile, had been impressed: He told his readers to rush right out and buy the Robert Hall Syrahs, because they were bargains.

Plenty of people at the gift shop were doing just that. Something told me I was about to spend time at the kind of winery I usually avoid. It's not that great wine *can't* be made in a modern facility where the winemaker isn't the owner—it's just that great wines rarely emerge from this situation. When I noticed a pack of people from Gallo's Rancho Zabacco brand, I suspected the wines would be a disaster. When I saw a happy shopper with a *Sideways* baseball cap, I knew it without a doubt.

Yet, as I saw that my host, Don Brady, was an open, generous sort of man, I tried to feel the same toward his wines as we headed down into the cool, cool winery to taste. On the way, he told me how lucky he was because he got to work with such beautiful grapes. Ever since I had eaten from Big Joe's Tree of Knowledge and embraced the wine skeptic within, I never believed a word winemakers told me unless I was able to taste and size up for myself whether the wine was made with indigenous yeasts. For confirmation of my suspicions, I would then innocently say, "Wow, that's something. What strain of yeast do you use?" I grilled winemakers about everything else as well.

The tasting ritual in Paso Robles began with a sip and a spit. My brain flashed to another item posted on the Web site:

43

Today, Robert Hall Winery is the result of an old-fashioned work ethic combined with traditional winemaking techniques and new state-of-the-art equipment. All grapes are hand-harvested in small, select lots. Fruit is handled as little as possible and each barrel is constantly monitored.

Yet I felt as if I were being poisoned. Something was grabbing me at the back of my throat. Bad acid adjustment? Pencil-like tannins, highly unnatural tasting, choked me. The wine tampering was so obvious that I wanted to engage Don in a conversation about what he meant by *traditional* techniques. Crushing grapes?

Soon, I felt I could identify the techniques he had used to create the wine—acidulation, tannin addition, that sort of thing. I started to ask more directed questions. Mr. Brady, eager to tell me about his love affair with tannin adjustment, said, "I like using ones [tannins] from chestnut."

Brady went on, "I put everything in the wine at the beginning: acid, tannin, wood chips, enzymes. That way, I can take things out instead of adding them later. It's like making a rich soup." I had a vision of a mad chef throwing all sorts of ingredients into the fermenter.

Then Brady started to draw molecular diagrams to illustrate the wisdom of using chestnut tannin to fix color and structure. I was too shocked to remember to ask whether he used any machines, but after I left I realized: Of course he at least used reverse osmosis. After all, he'd told me, "That way I can take things out . . ."

Oh, that soup.

While Brady did not go to University of California, Davis, School of Enology and Viticulture to study, his approach to winemaking, leaving nothing up to nature, is the industry standard. And the fact that he never questions what is—or is not—natural about his winemaking is also status quo. I had to stop and wonder: Why was winemaking taught this way? Why was there a huge gap between my reality and the industry's? Why wasn't romance and artistry part of the process? Wanting to see where all this desire for control emanated from, I felt it imperative to pay a visit to the professors who teach about ninety percent of winemakers in the United States and plenty of winemakers worldwide.

Davis has been in the business of educating winemakers in their trade for more than a hundred years. I won't say that there has never been an instance where I loved the wine of one of their graduates, but such a case is rare. Most of the winemakers I love learned from their father, grandfather, or mother. Yet Davis is a reference and can lay claim to being one of the top, if not *the* top, wine schools in the world. I saw it as essential to explore their approach to wine teaching—and what they were doing that was so wrong, from my perspective.

Soon, I was rolling my bag off of a plane and toward the waiting Professor Roger Boulton. Taller than I had expected, he was a courtly Australian, with a strong signature: a thick, almost Nietzschelike mustache.

I was caught off guard when he promptly approached me. I asked how he'd recognized me. He reminded me about the many photos posted on my blog. I suppose that not recognizing my red hair would be like missing the fur on his upper lip. On the way to campus, I brought up Clark Smith of Vinovation.

"He was a student of yours, no?"

"Yes," he said.

I searched for some expression under the mustache to signal what he really thought. Getting none, I launched into a query. "I had an e-mail exchange with him last week about the reverse-osmosis process," I began. "He told me he's found yet another great use of the machine, the production of a Pinot-Noir monomeric tannin concentrate that enhances flavor and color extraction from skins when added to fermentation. He says that this little secret is now used by a dozen or so of the top Pinot producers. So," I asked, "he extracts pigment from the skins of the Pinot Noir grape and then adds it to fermenting Pinot?"

A hint of emotion blistered under the mustache. Much of Professor Boulton's research is on this topic. "Yes," he said. "What he says is correct." He got annoyed, continuing, "I get upset when I hear about someone's 'new idea.' There are very few new ideas. This is all flavor of the month. It's almost like everyone else before us was too stupid to realize the truth about making wine. It's very frustrating. Traditions are there for a reason."

The tradition Boulton was talking about was the ancient tradition of cofermenting some white grapes when making red wine. For centuries, some white grapes were blended in with the red grapes for Chianti, but now this practice is rare. The aromatic white grape Viognier is still added to some wines of the northern

Rhône. Though counterintuitive, the practice enhances color. Boulton said it was cheaper and simpler than using the reverse-osmosis machine for the same desired effect.

"I've been around long enough to know," he said, "that you don't interview the hotshot new winemaker or consultant. Instead, ask the grandfather who did it before technology. Then you'll see the real answer."

I've been interviewing Boulton since 2001 and have always enjoyed talking with him because of his directness as well as his encyclopedic knowledge of the wine-making world and its history. When he talks this way, about learning from the old-timers, I almost think he's on my side of the debate.

Boulton is extremely protective of Davis. His attachment to the school is strong. Filled with pride, he showed me the huge oak conference table, a present from Seguin Moreau, the French barrel maker. In the corner of the conference room was a photograph Ansel Adams took of the UC Davis wine cellar in 1966. "The cellar looks like it did in the 1920s," Boulton told me. "You'll see." He guided me down to the cellar, and I saw he was right. The room was exactly the same, with wooden shelves for bottles and lots of glass demijohns for experiments.

The contrast was startling. The wine-making facilities were so low-tech. So bare bones. Yet the way the faculty teaches students to make wine is so modern and high-tech. Who knows what winemaking will be like when the school launches its state-of-the-art Maynard A. Amerine Teaching and Research Winery?

Why pussyfoot around? I thought. *Why not just get into it?* "Why," I asked, "doesn't the school teach natural winemaking?"

I can see now that my delivery wasn't great. I started with the assumption that they were screwing up, so how could his reception be other than frosty?

"We teach science, not personal preferences or philosophy, and we try to avoid teaching the obvious. 'Natural' gives variable results and inconsistent flavor. We teach the science of winemaking. We don't teach a style."

Boulton's response was a mystery to me because I view natural winemaking as a method, not a style. Why not teach natural winemaking as a viable path?

To be fair, techniques taught in other schools seem more nefarious. For example, Davis doesn't teach winemakers to add enzymes to hold and stabilize color (among other things), but other schools do. "I can't find any proof that they work," Boulton explained, "so we don't teach students how to use them."

I wondered how it was possible that enzyme use is so prevalent in the industry if wine students are not taught how to use them in school?

"Most winemakers are being informed what these products do by the suppliers," he said.

"Just like pharmaceutical companies try to get my brother the doctor to use cholesterol-reducing drugs?" I asked.

The answer was yes.

While Boulton came out all for tannin addition to adjust a mouthfeel, he was outraged when companies who produce tannins make claims that they are good for fixing sun-damaged fruit or unripe grape tannins, modifying aromas, improving aging potential, and stabilizing red wine color.

Next he segued into ethics. "How can we talk about ripe tannins," he asked, "if they come from the measuring cup and not from the grape? This is a question of integrity."

Now, Boulton doesn't care what is added, as long as there is no deception. He asks that claims be supported by science. He also beats the drum for wine-making transparency and a consumer wine law. He advocates for all additives and processes out of the norm to be listed on wine labels. The next additive up for debate, he told me, was liquid oak extract, previously legal only for home winemaking.

"Do what you want to do, but put it on the label—please," he argued in his strong Australian twang. "In a trial the witness is called. If the attorney doesn't ask the right question and the witness doesn't offer the evidence, is that lying? Is withholding knowledge ever honorable?"

It's hard to believe that the industry wouldn't fight transparency with every bit of muscle it has. I just don't see Big Wine allowing labels on wine reading something like this: *This wine was de-alcoholized by reverse osmosis and smoothed out with micro-oxygenation. Ingredients: Water, alcohol, grapes, chestnut tannin, oak extract, oak dust, genetically modified yeast, urea, enzymes, grape juice, tartaric acid, bentonite, and Velcorin.*

On a naturally made wine, the ingredient list would read simply: *Grapes and minimal sulfur (100 parts per million or lower).*

Boulton deposited me in the cramped office of Dr. Douglas Adams, professor of vineyard management. While Adams is not the head irrigation guy (Larry E. Williams is), irrigation is his domain because it is part of the way today's winemakers ripen grapes. I had contact with Dr. Williams for a story I wrote on irrigation after I became obsessed with challenging its use when observing irrigation pipes in rainy Oregon vineyards. California was arid, parched; I could understand its need to water. But in Oregon?

I learned that drip irrigation was perfected by the Israelis for growing crops in the desert. Drip irrigation (to the tune of five thousand dollars an acre) first started to spread through California in the 1970s. Roots that previously had to dig deep in order to survive now hung out close to the surface of the ground—and that's where Williams likes them. He'd told me, "If you're a grape grower, you want to have that vine dependent on what you do so you can manipulate it."

In human romance, such manipulative behavior might be sufficient reason to consult the nearest couples' therapist; for a vineyard manager it is part of a supposedly healthy, co-dependent relationship. Hearing Williams expound on the connection between an irrigator and his vine roots was extremely creepy but his theory epitomized something I came to view as a great flaw in the UC Davis mentality and the world wine-school gestalt: a desire for complete dominance and control.

Consider the nature of a grapevine, a highly efficient life form when it comes to finding water. The people who make the wines I love are those who seek the expression of *terroir* and who often believe grapes are merely a medium to channel soil minerality and weather. This is why regions with incredibly complex soils that produce inimitable wines (like Burgundy and Piedmont) are so revered. To be special, though, the grapevines must have healthy, strong roots that carve deep down into the earth. The best grapes come from plants grown on interesting soil whose vines drill through all sorts of porous or dense mineral to find a water source. (Some winemakers claim to have seen roots that can drill down sixty feet.) If a region gets significant rain, say nineteen inches a year, irrigation is not essential. If you hedge your bets and irrigate, the vines' roots stay close to the surface and never get to suck up the soil's complexity and deliver it to the fruit. In other words, the roots will have very little to say to the grapes. In wine or in love, that kind of lapse in connection and communication is not my thing.

Irrigation was in place when the root-eating louse phylloxera hit California vineyards in the late 1980s. Growers replanted, deciding to spurn the drought-resistant rootstock most of California had been planted on. In its place they used riparian rootstock—water-loving stuff. The other part of the equation was their mimicry of tight, Bordeaux-vineyard-style spacing: up to 2,500 vines per acre instead of 450, the status quo. All of this increased irrigation requirements to as high as 100 to 200 gallons of water per vine per season, a significant jump in a state with severe water deficits.

Frog's Leap is one of Napa Valley's first organic wineries. Owner/vintner John Williams told me that when he started the winery in 1987 he looked out at the dry-farmed vines he'd bought and said to himself, "Hell, I'm a graduate of UC Davis and by golly, we know how to take care of a vineyard! Irrigate!" He soon realized that he was killing his vines. He quickly stopped irrigating and returned to dry farming. And he sidestepped the plague of the root-eating phylloxera. John Williams and others have wondered whether irrigating drought-resistant rootstock brought on the phylloxera debacle. The possibility has never been studied, but has been outright dismissed by UC Davis's Larry Williams.

Irrigation not only keeps the vine well hydrated; it's also a significant player in fruit manipulation. Since the early 1990s, the fashion has been to pick grapes at high Brix, the measure used for grape sugar—and irrigation has a role here. Phillip Coturri, whose vineyard management company, Enterprise Vineyards, operates mostly in Napa and Sonoma, is in demand for his organic farming skill. He put it this way: "Remember eucalyptus and green-bean flavors? Those were due to unripe grapes. To get today's superripe flavors, the vines need hydration. Irrigation produces a very different type of wine. Irrigation is a tool to extend ripening."

So I was eager to meet with Doug Adams to talk irrigation. The professor seemed nervous to meet me, though. I could imagine Honey-Sugar greeting him with a joke, something like, "Is that an irrigation pipe or are you just happy to see me?" Instead, he motioned for me to sit down, I laid off the jokes, and he (unbidden) started to tell me how he sees a lot of student winemakers looking to be Parker's next darlings, how winemaker has become the new celebrity chef, the new rock star. His students craved fame.

"It's all about Parker, isn't it?" Adams sighed.

"Pretty much," I told him.

"Not the *Wine Spectator*?" he asked.

"A close second," I said.

"Jancis Robinson?" he asked, referring to the marvelous British wine writer.

"I wish," I said. "Few in America know who she is. She doesn't rate wine on a hundred-point scale. Even if people don't know Parker, they see the points."

"Okay," Adams said then, leaning back on his swivel chair. "Let's go. Though I don't know if I have anything to tell you."

"Are you kidding?" I told him. "You've got tons to tell. Just tons. For example, let's talk irrigation."

Apparently, he wasn't prepared for this question from a city-based, fire-escape-gardening New Yorker. He started by saying that because the New World notion is to plant anywhere and have technology fill in where nature doesn't, plenty of land plots that have no water source are used for vineyards—ergo, the drip is essential.

"Well, what about being more careful and growing grapes where you don't need to irrigate?" I asked. "What about the Old World model of site first and grapes second?"

He was already amused with me, that I could see. I continued.

"Sometimes I think the New World is like a spoiled child with an undeveloped superego, wanting everything fast, unable to wait. It took centuries of observation to find out which grape tasted best from which plot of soil in the Old World; the New World can start making its own observations. What about Napa? Like in Oakville—the flat land on the highway? Do you think they have to irrigate?"

Adams told me probably not. But to stop, growers would have to rip out the newer, tightly spaced vines and replant with the old, drought-resistant rootstock.

Hearing this, I recalled a dinner I'd had with the winemaker of Opus One, the famous first joint venture between Mouton Roth-schild and Robert Mondavi.

Adams laughed when I brought this up. He had his own story about Mr. Opus One Winemaker. "I read that he irrigated by 'stressing' the vine," he told me. "But he wouldn't stress it enough to put the vine into a 'panic.' Now we're ascribing emotions and personalities to plants?"

I didn't mind ascribing personalities and emotions to plants at all. Anyone who has a garden might feel similarly. But when the Opus winemaker told me (proudly) that he was weaning his vines off the drip, I asked him, "When will they be totally off?"

He said never, it was impossible.

I then told him that his neighbor, Grgich Hills Winery, didn't irrigate.

He stubbornly repeated, "Napa is a desert."

The day after our dinner, I called Grgich's winemaker, Ivo Jera-maz. Ivo's uncle, Mike Grgich, who founded the winery and vineyard, learned to farm in Croatia, so when he arrived in California, he knew not to irrigate. I asked Ivo what he thought of Mr. Opus One Winemaker's insistence that the vines needed to be watered.

Impatiently, in his stiff Croatian accent, Ivo asked, "How did our grandfathers manage without irrigation? They are so brainwashed, these winemakers, with their chemicals. If you have irrigated and used chemicals for fifteen years, you will see devastation in your vineyard. Those vines are addicted to the drip. Their root system is destroyed."

Adams seemed to enjoy this story, but in the way he might enjoy using his grandmother's remedy for a sore throat. It was quaint. He responded, "The old ways were based on an intuition that science and technology now ignore. I love it when we find someone who knows all about how our grandfathers used to do things and why. Observations remain. Explanations for the observations may change, and then change again." Adams told me that he admires intuition but he can't teach it, or teach his students to listen to it. They will have to find out about intuition on their own.

I appreciated that Adams and Boulton talked about going to the elders to find out how they solved problems. But I wondered: Then why didn't UC Davis offer a class in Old World solutions to New World problems? You can't be accepted to the Yale drama school if you don't have some sort of inner artistic fire. How could the world's leading institution for wine education fail to recognize the indispensability of intuition, the need for talent in its students? I felt that perhaps with a little push Adams could be convinced. He seemed a bit disparaging about modern wine-making, calling it "stylistic determination."

"We have learned how to turn the knob, and it's hard to go back," he said. "It's like how we learned to take the bell-pepper flavor out of Cabernet Franc." I was encouraged to notice a little sadness in his voice in mentioning the removal of that taste in Cabernet Franc, which Parker is said not to care for. Another element affected by the turn of the knob—thanks to irrigation—was grape sweetness.

Back in the days when I enjoyed California wine, 23 to 24 on the Brix scale was considered terrific ripeness. But by the early 1990s Parker started giving huge, up-to-perfect scores for sugary, flabby wines. The ultraripe flavor I attributed to Helen Turley became the rage, then virtually the standard, ruining the flavor and spunk of the Zinfandels and the other California wines I sometimes enjoyed. Winemakers started to claim that "ripeness" was not achieved at a low Brix and started to pick when the grapes were near 30 Brix. And irrigation helps the grapes get there. In my darker moments I liken the manipulative approach to fattening a duck for its foie. The process caters to the world's sweet tooth, which in turn fomented the Yellow Tail fiasco. Yellow Tail, a cheap wine from Australia, is one of the best-selling wines in the United States. In the car heading to campus, Roger Boulton had summed up Yellow Tail's success this way: "It gives a lot of sugary flavor with a chewy texture at a low price point." I'd bet money on research being able to prove that wine is good for your health, but wines that are overripe and sugary, like Yellow Tail and its imitators, are not.

The trend to pick later and later for riper and riper grapes not only makes for sloppy wine, but it also blurs the differences between the grape varieties and causes all sorts of *tzuris* in the winery. Nature just doesn't want to make wine when the grapes are so ripe. When grapes come in at such high Brix, they have a hard time finishing their fermentation. To make sure the wine finishes, winemakers use added yeast and yeast food (based on urea)— otherwise, the yeasts won't have enough muscle to eat those heavy sugars. Even these techniques are no guarantee, and winemakers might lose a batch. That's when they reach for the reverse-osmosis machine to help out. They reach for the machine again to bring down the alcohol level. Or perhaps they add water instead, to dilute the wine. By this point the wine is so flabby that it has to be rebuilt with added tannins and acidulation. You get the picture.

I decided to try a slightly different tack with Adams. Because he is in charge of farming, and biodynamic farming was becoming the buzzword in the industry, I had to ask, "Aren't your students interested?"

"Of course they're interested. But we're not teaching it." That refusal seemed a little stubborn, as vineyards worldwide were and are carrying out experiments to test the validity of biodynamics. Then again, how could I expect a scientific institution to take seriously a regimen that includes burying a horn filled with cow dung on the winter solstice, digging it up on the vernal equinox, and then diluting it to use as fertilizer? Adams looked at me as if I really had gone off my rocker. He answered directly, though. "Because everyone is talking about it, I wanted to understand," he said. "I read Joly's book *From Vine to Earth*. I know the theory now."

"And that would be?" I asked.

"Taking natural phenomena, like different phases of the planets and the moon, into account and farming organically accordingly." Joly lost Adams with the phases. "I don't see how the phases of the planets and moon could have anything to do with plant physiology. I really can't find any proof. It's a little like saying you want your plant to be stressed but not panicked."

In full, vivid Technicolor, I saw the problem. "You're all scientists here!" I blurted out. My statement elicited quite a look of puzzlement on Adams's face.

"But we are still people!" he answered. "When you study science they don't remove a part of your brain, you know."

I hesitated. I pondered.

"Is there some doubt about that, Alice?" Adams asked.

I had no doubt about that, but I did wonder what sort of personalities were attracted to this line of work. I began to explore a tentative theory. "Have you considered that you became a scientist because the part of your brain that needs absolute proof is overdeveloped?" I began. "I am wired in the opposite way. I trust the empirical more than the absolute. There's nothing I can do about it. But you were born that way, the way I was born this way. When you were two years old, weren't you organizing your toys analytically?" I asked.

"Oh, no," he said.

"But you were probably very young when you started to say, 'Prove it.'"

That got him. Adams backtracked. "Forget about proof," he said, "think of it as I'm looking for the best explanation. Winemakers are acute observers. But with biodynamics, scientists can't extrapolate from the observations because the explanations are so screwy. So, phases of the moon? Tell me your observations. What's the best explanation? If it includes the moon, so be it. But I bet we can find a better explanation than the moon."

At the end of the day, after a walk through the cork tree–lined streets of Davis, I brought up biodynamic wines with Boulton. My question elicited the most disdain of any I had asked him that day. His thick brush of a mustache quivered. Or did I just imagine it?

"Biodynamic wines are better?" he scoffed. "Please, show me. Give me twenty people on a panel and have them see the difference. Line up one hundred wines that you know are organic or biodynamic. Line up another hundred that are not. Please. In a blind tasting. Please. Get me twenty people on a panel, and tell me if they can tell the difference. For Pete's sake, show me, don't tell me. Prove it to me."

But is this the kind of thing that can be proved? This is about taste preference. The taste of biodynamic and organic and natural is one that appeals to a whole slew of people. The taste of the other kind of wine, one that I view more as a beverage than an art, appeals to another group. Shouldn't both kinds of wine-making be taught?

"Upsettingly, biodynamics is on the verge of becoming a marketing platform." I went on. "I can see the day when even Gallo will issue a biodynamic wine because it would be good for their image. But up to now, winemakers and drinkers have come to biodynamic or natural or authentic wines purely because they do taste better and not because of some advertising campaign. I don't see how you can ignore this kind of force. Now, are you playing devil's advocate with me? You don't really think that wine filled with chemicals and additives can taste better, do you?"

He repeated, "Don't tell me, show me"—but this time, did he say it with a twinkle? I wonder if the scientists on the UC Davis faculty have ever had enough of my kind of wines in their tasting repertoire to come to an informed opinion. I think these wine-loving scientists who teach the next generation may not know how fabulous the wines I drink can be. Might these two professors evolve in the tradition of so many scientists who after decades of denying God due to lack of proof, became intensely spiritual and in later years decide that perhaps my ideas for teaching winemaking weren't so crazy?

I had very little time left with Professor Boulton before I had to scoot out to the airport and I wanted to take our conversation a bit further. "What did your parents do?" I asked.

He was stunned by my personal question. I saw he took it as traipsing on turf where I didn't belong. But instead of telling me, as I feared he would, that it was none of my business, he good-naturedly answered. He was the only one of his siblings to have gone for an education. Neither father nor mother graduated high school and, he said with tremendous pride, "My father was a tradesman, in the shoe industry. He was the best there was."

"I suppose he had a very exacting personality?"

Boulton said yes. He clearly adored his father. But, still, he seemed uncomfortable with my trespass. I was not playing by the rules; I had crossed into the personal. I had also hit a nerve. "Why did you want to know?" he asked.

"I wanted to find out what makes a scientist need proof when the proof in the glass should be enough," I answered.

"Well, did you find out?" he asked.

"I found out something consistent with the rest of human development; it's a little nature and a little nurture."

I headed to the airport and cogitated on the Davis problem. When Louis Pasteur got involved with yeast, he unwittingly laid the groundwork for the industry to pass out of the hands of farmers and into the realm of scientists. A winemaker needs tools, after all. But I believe that technology, science, and business had squelched the creativity, immediacy, and urgency once inherent to winemaking. In their place was correctness and control. This is not my way in love and not the kind of wine I want, either. As I reached the Sacramento airport I thought, *What they need in this school is a philosopher or two. That would fix everything.*

– 3 –

Putting Syrah on the Couch

To me, the Syrah grape of the northern Rhône can be like Stanley Kowalski after therapy; muscular and intense but with an intellect to match its sexuality and sometimes even a willingness to show kindness to animals. A bad-boy grape worth saving. We all have had at least one Stanley in our lives, and mine was the Owl Man.

Though I fell in love with the Owl Man instantly, I was always aware of the delicate infrastructure of his darkness. Similarly, with Syrah, I sometimes sensed a skunklike aroma beneath its wild blackberry fruit, racehorse muscle, and mineral charm from the granite and limestone soil. Both the man and the grape had extraordinary qualities, though it took a lot of work to get to them.

I'll save the conjecture about how the Owl Man got that way for my novel, but what made Syrah that way? The skunky smell could have been from too much sulfur added in an overzealous attempt to keep the wine stable. In the absence of oxygen, Syrah, more than, say, Pinot Noir, tends to produce off odors similar to rotten eggs or skunk. This is called reduction. A little bit of skunk is fine, lots of skunk, bad. Often, the wine just needs time to settle or air out.

But Syrah—silty, magical Syrah, in all its contradictions— reminds me of something that happened the first time I took the Owl Man to my friend Becky's house in Bouilland, Burgundy. I was reading on a bench, on a dusty day, while Becky's neighbor was grooming horses. The air around me was filled with a sensual, powdery smell. An hour later I had the worst allergy attack of my life. I was covered with hives from inhaling all that dander. I find it an interesting metaphor for the kind of pain I experienced when the Owl Man and I separated.

I spent eleven years with him. The demise of our relationship coincided with the birthday that ushered me solidly into middle age, and that summer I did what the Victorians used to do: I took to the continent to heal my heart. My plan was to visit the northern Rhône to get intimate with Syrah on its home turf. I half hoped I'd fall in love with some wild and woolly maker of incredibly pure wines and live out my midlife crisis in style. On the other hand, if I came to terms with Syrah, perhaps I could accept my loss. I have been known to have peculiar logic before. This was one of those times. I wasn't in my right mind.

Syrah, known as Shiraz in Australia, is the noble red grape of the northern Rhône Valley. There are plenty of legends surrounding its origin. One story credits the Phoenicians of Asia

Minor with bringing the grape to France from Shiraz, Persia, when they established Marseilles around 600 BC. Another story claims that Romans brought the varietal from Syracuse, in Sicily, in the third century AD. These days, popular thinking has it that it and its close grape relations, Mondeuse and Durif, are Rhône natives.

No matter where it came from, Syrah was established in the vineyards surrounding the Rhône village of Tain l'Hermitage by the thirteenth century. In the 1650s, South Africa became the first country outside of France to plant Syrah. It showed up in Australia, where it is called Shiraz, at the end of the eighteenth century, and became the country's most planted grape. I have found one—count 'em—one Shiraz in all of Australia that I actually like. This is Castagna. After I tasted it, I learned that it was grown biodynamically. Unlike most wines from Australia, Castagna has no perceptible new oak and the grapes are not pushed to the limit of their ripeness. Interestingly enough, Julian Castagna calls his wine Syrah, not Shiraz. The vintner is eager to distance himself from the overblown, spoofulated Shirazes to which Robert Parker awards such enthusiastic copy and points. Once, at the end of a conversation, Parker said to me, "I suspect you're one of those who don't like Barossa Valley Shirazes?" He was correct there. The Barossa is known for flamboyant Shiraz like that 100-point three-hundred-dollar Three Rivers. When Parker told me I had to look beyond the points to his description, I did. But "explosive bouquet of crème de cassis, espresso, melted fudge"? Not a description that makes me want to hold out my glass for a pour. It might make me extend my spoon for some ice cream, though.

The first records of Syrah in the United States have it arriving in California in 1878, but it remained scarce here until quite recently. All too often the variety is grown so ripe that the gorgeous structure the grape can offer is lost and its nuances fall into vapid sweetness. Some Californians, who truly follow the acknowledged and acclaimed masters of the grapes in the Rhône—Allemand and Clape in Cornas, Chave in Hermitage—are onto something. I still have my doubts that California can produce a great Syrah, but at least there are some interesting wines coming from the hands of Steve Edmunds (Edmunds St. John) and Wells Guthrie (Copain Wine Cellars).

Most wine drinkers don't have a clue that the southern and northern parts of the Rhône are as different as the Confederacy was from the Union—so any diner who orders a Cornas thinking it's a "Rhône" and expecting a sun-kissed, semicooked, prune-filled wine is in for a big shock. The south grows thirteen red grapes and all are allowed in Chateauneuf-du-Pape, though the most celebrated grape there is the fleshy, sappy Grenache.

But in the north, the red-wine culture is all about mineral, horsey Syrah. There are five red wine–growing communes. Crozes-Hermitage, St.-Joseph, and Cornas are considered the most rustic. Hermitage and Côte-Rôtie are considered the most important. Parker prefers Hermitage and Côte-Rôtie: They get his highest points, are the most gentrified, and not surprisingly have more wines made with lots of new oak and forward fruit tricks. True to my peasant stock, I prefer the more edgy expressions of St.-Jo, Crozes, and Cornas. Though I've seen New World flavors infiltrate even the northern Rhône, thanks to stubbornness there is a smallish group of traditional winemakers not in danger of going over to the dark side. These more old-style winemakers prefer to use grape stems during fermentation, and of course they don't inoculate with yeast or do any of the fancy technical stuff. They might use large barrels or small barrels, but there is hardly any new oak and there are certainly no additives.

Though I wanted to take my post–Owl Man Rhône journey by my lonesome, it wasn't meant to be. The Skinny Food Writer wanted to meet me. My friend Skinny and I had traveled so many times together by this point that we had our own secret language for wine. She knew what I meant when I said "puppy's breath," or "bloody," and I knew what she meant when she described a wine as "chicken soup," or "rusty nail." We have a similar rhythm, and rarely get into fights. She is invaluable as a navigator and she eats meat, which covers up for the fact that I don't. She was also newly separated from her husband, and I didn't have the heart to say no.

But then she sprang an unwelcome surprise. She was saddled with an old friend of hers, a towering blond woman in wine sales. This was a narcissistic, perpetually late, Manolo-mule-, push-up-bra-, and essential-oil–wearing yoga princess of a woman, the kind of girl my mother would have called Miss Knish. An odd trio we were. The smelly femme fatale, the happily liberated, and me, a still raw, thin-to-the-bone woman who just wanted a very solo adventure. Together, with me in the driver's seat, we sped along-side the Rhône.

The Rhône River starts as a wee thing in Switzerland and then gathers strength when it hits France. The entire river stretches 125 miles, forty of which sluice the middle of the vineyards that mark the northern Rhône. We drove it until we hit the first major wine town, Ampuis. I gazed up in wonder at the steep hills of Côte-Rôtie, at the vines that were trellised like beanpoles. This vertical positioning is called *échalas*. As Côte-Rôtie melted into St.-Joseph, the overcast weather burned off and it was as hot as July in the Sinai. *This is what they call cool-climate Syrah?* I wondered. If I couldn't breathe, how could the grapes? Then the apricots began. The road was lined with the fruit trees. Unable to contain myself, I pulled over and gathered us a few. Their skins tight as the head of a banjo, the fruit gushed upon puncture of tooth. These weren't one-dimensional, sugary flavors. The sweet was tempered by a splash of salt, by depth. I felt as if I had just broken a fast. Food tasted good again.

The apricots were a revelation, and so was drinking Chave's older Hermitage in the estate's cellar. The Chaves are considered the area's First Family. The domaine has been passed from father to son since 1481, and the black, cottony mycelium growing on the walls in their cellar looks as if it's been around just as long. Parker likes these wines as well as I do, and included Chave in his book *World's Greatest Wine Estates*. He also thinks, however, that the wines got better when the son, Jean-Louis, returned from studying at UC Davis. The wines are gorgeous, no doubt.

Spectacular. The tasting was remarkable. Luckily for us, the older Chave, Gérard, had just returned from Canada. When Gérard returns home he likes to taste through an array of wines, in the way a returning parent may pet the heads of his children. We were treated to lots of just-opened older vintages. I don't think I have ever been in a more freezing cellar. It was over a hundred degrees outside, but down among the bottles my fingers were turning white. Even with the California experience that Parker thinks did so much good, Jean-Louis said the words I would hear from all winemakers who make wines I love to drink: "You cannot inoculate a wine with industrial yeast and talk of *terroir* and you can't talk of *terroir* if you talk of planting your land with clones from a nursery." Hearing these beliefs from the younger generation of winemakers, those who had the sense and wisdom not to reinvent the wheel, would drive home again and again what Doug Adams at UC Davis told me—"There were plenty of wonderful wines before science came along"—as well as Roger Boulton's words, "You have to look to the grandfathers."

On our way out, Jean-Louis handed us a half bottle of wine called *vin de paille,* saying, "You're going to see George tonight? Please, give this to him." The 1996 was the first vintage his father let him make. *Vin de paille* is a rare, expensive sweet wine made from grapes dried to raisins on straw mats. It takes five years to finish its fermentation, and the 1996 was finally ready. If he did not believe in making wine naturally, Jean-Louis would have sped through the fermentation in a tenth of the time.

Our hotel was in part owned by winemaker Michel Chapoutier, one of the Big Men in Town. When we first walked in, we were shocked that such a Gucci-loafer kind of guy would own such a dump of a hotel. Nevertheless, I was happy to go horizontal for an hour—even between thin, scratchy sheets with an air conditioner that seemed to be running on mouse power. Around ten o'clock, when the sun and the heat went down and the wind picked up, we walked across the narrow road to the wine store run by George the Greek. George is one of those mythic characters, manic, warm, and welcoming. Next to the mostly stony northern Rhône folk, he was like a hot tub on a cold day. Playing host, George showed us our seats at the tables he had set up in the gutter outside of the store. There we were joined by a few winemakers and their wives, who were eating George's homemade paté and *saucisson*. Champagne arrived, made by Anselme Selosse, the crazy guy from Champagne who showed that it was possible to work organically in the area. He was the first of the acclaimed independent vignerons in Champagne. His was a cult Champagne, very rare, but George seemed to have a never-ending supply. Our companions were polite to us, and they shared their wine.

I met the silent, unfriendly Laurent Combier. The most dazzling of his wines was a 1995 Crozes-Hermitage his father had made. I was not fond of the wine from the younger man's hand, and here's why. Combier said, "In a bad year I use no oak, and in a good year I use a lot of oak." If that's the case, and I know it is, I would only drink his wines in disasterous years like 2002. At the table we also met a tall apricot farmer and winemaker named Florent Viale. He had a too-stinky-to-assess Domaine du Colombier Hermitage. Our Miss Knish flirted and contemplated an affair with Mikus, George's macho, extremely handsome nephew. "I'm sending out the vibe." She giggled. "I can feel it. I haven't been vibe sending for years." It all struck me as unseemly. At three-thirty in the morning, we noticed that almost six hours had passed. That's when it hit me: This wasn't a wine bar but George's nightly party. *How does he not go broke?* I wondered. We stood up to begin the short walk across the street to the roach motel when George remembered the sweet wine, which we had never drunk. He insisted we show up in the morning for breakfast.

Four and a half hours later, we three were ministered to by the men, neither of whom looked as ragged as we felt. The incredibly fresh and energetic George and Mikus plied us with croissants, the local challahlike bread called Pogne, and fresh orange juice. While waiting for the espresso machine to fire up, George popped the bottle of *vin de paille*. Pure and sweetly tart, it tasted of apricot nectar. This was the first time I would ever drink a 235-dollar half bottle of wine—for breakfast—and not spit. We rode off with a taste of the silky wine in our mouths, leaving the mysteries of Syrah behind for another time.

It's not that I didn't get anything out of that first trip to further my understanding of Syrah, or the Owl Man. I met winemakers on my shortlist of greats besides Chave. In Cornas, with its vine-lined bowls of land, so difficult to work, so rocky, I saw that working the area takes a specific kind of person—one who, like the Owl Man, thrives on impossible tasks. This work seemed to squeeze big, sueded tannins and dusty licorice out of the stubborn, edgy wine. In Cornas, I met the Clapes, Auguste and his son Pierre Marie, who stolidly resisted all New World influence, including the use of small barrels. Instead, they use large, old, oval ones, like the *foudres* used for Alsatian wines. Practically across the street was Thierry Allemand, who, like almost every other handsome winemaker I met, was going through a divorce. When I tasted his wines, so beautiful, especially from his older vines, I had a momentary thought of being the next Madame Allemand. But he wasn't asking. And I was probably not sending out the Miss Knish kind of vibe. Being a renegade, he talked with wonder about his visit to California for a festival in Paso Robles, Hospice de Rhône.

"The winemakers there tasted my wines and asked, 'What are your acidities? What are your pH's?' When I answered, 'Who knows?' they couldn't believe it."

Like many of the wineries I visited, there were no labs to test the wine chemistry. All was done by taste and instinct. Allemand took one full year to properly learn how to knot the straw to tie the vines to the poles to train in that *echalas* style. Any California winemaker I meet will tell me that his wine is made in the vineyard, but I'd like to meet the California winemaker who would spend a year learning to tie a knot.

I also realized that the skunk I often smelled in Syrah, as long as it wasn't too overpowering, could be like the balance between pleasure and pain. As my dentist once told me when explaining how to use a dental pick, "Push into the gums until you feel a pain that almost feels good." Yes, there were plenty of similarities to life with the Owl Man.

I was onto something, but even with this peek into the soul of Syrah, I couldn't lay claim to real understanding. That would have to wait. After all, one can't recover from heartbreak in a mere few months, and it takes more than one visit to a wine region to snuggle into its soul.

What is this stuff about a wine region, a grape, and soul, anyway? I have never visited Australia, so I don't know if that country has a soul to express through the Syrah grape. Based on the wines I have tasted, I imagine that there's an awful lot of bad karma to expunge before the soul can be free. In the late 1990s, the Australians flooded the international wine market with "flavor" and "texture"—capital F, capital T. Great and popular are rarely the same thing. But popular always gets imitated. Now, seeking the mass market, *Shiraz* sometimes appears on the wine labels of France, as in Fat Bastard Shiraz. I feel like shaking these wine bottles by the shoulders and yelling, It's Syrah, not Shiraz, bubba!

The European Union isn't helping matters by asking its winemakers to study the New World success and make adjustments accordingly. The EU wants simpler labeling, wants the varietal on the label (even though so many wines are blends). It wants winemakers to use oak chips and flavor-flouncing tricks. This kind of thinking reminds me of when a college professor told me that, if I wanted to write literature, I could learn nothing from bad writing. In France, if the right people are tapped, there are not only 150 years of wine-making history to draw from, but there is also a vast infrastructure of unparalleled observational wisdom. These are things the New World does not have. There are times when the newcomer has an answer or two, there are times when the old dogs can learn a new trick or two—but really, why would anyone from France go to Australia to learn about Syrah? (And some are doing this.) How did the newcomer come to set the benchmark for the grape?

THE ONLY THING good about Miss Knish's coming along on that Rhône journey was her introducing me to Francesco Pimpinella, who, in addition to being a winemaker and consultant, scouts wines for a small American wine importer. Francesco reminds me of an enthusiastic Russian wolfhound. A tall, overgrown-boylike man, everything about him is endearing. When I wanted to return to the Rhône, Francesco said he would offer me shelter, one day of his time, and his translation skills.

When I did head back to the Rhône, it was with a significantly healed heart. Zipping along the highway, I watched the soft white limestone soil where Pinot Noir thrives give way to the crushed granite that makes the world's best Syrah. For my new friend, I had two visit requests. One was to visit a winemaker making a true New World wine, Australia-wannabe-style. The other was to visit the mysterious winemakers whose wines I adored, Dard et Ribo.

Francesco, his wife, and the two little Pimpinellas live in a cement house on the Rhône River in Tournon. Plain on the outside, spacious and airy on the inside, the house has a dramatic view of Hermitage Hill. Francesco's garden is worthy of the Neapolitan man he is, with a kiwi-draped shade arbor, pomegranate and apricot trees. Hungry for the taste, I was happy to be back in the land of apricots.

At sunset, we had the kind of meal that tempts me to buy a one-way ticket to France and join the ranks of ex-pats. The table was covered with cucumbers, olives, tomato tart, and wild-yeasted bread, which Francesco makes every other day.

"Tell me," Francesco said, "why did you want to see these people, Dard et Ribo?

"*Did?* Oh, my God, Francesco. We don't have an appointment?" I was panicked. "I have to see them. It's essential. I must meet them."

"Don't worry, Alice," he tried to calm me. "But, tell me, why do you want to go?" he repeated. "They are not important. I don't know these wines."

René Dard and François Ribo met in winemaking school and teamed up in 1984. Their homebase was in lowly Crozes-Hermitage, but they did have some more prestigious plots of land in Hermitage, not far from the Chave estate. When they started out, they worked conventionally, but soon they became convinced that making wine naturally, without overt intervention or the preservative sulfur, made a prettier, purer wine. These were the first wines made without sulfur (or with just a small spritz at bottling) I ever tasted, though at the time I had no idea how they were made. I just adored them. I first found their St.-Joseph and Crozes-Hermitage in New York. When I returned to buy them again, they had disappeared. I rediscovered their striking black label in Paris wine bars with Skinny, and then their wine became "our wine." I wanted the wines stateside. The adoring public was clamoring. Thankfully, Big Joe was investigating a way to import them again.

The Rhône has three other winemakers I know of who belong to the unofficial *sans soufre* club. They are motivated by the same belief: that the purest and truest wines are made without adding sulfur. These hardcores include a protégé of D & R, the gentle Hervé Souhaut in the Ardeche and St.-Joseph, the stony Thierry Allemand of Cornas, and the thoughtful Jean Michel Stephan in Côte-Rôtie.

The wines of Dard et Ribo absolutely had a purity, and aliveness and a way of changing with every sip and sniff, making them a really fun ride. I felt I needed to learn something about the humans who made them. But instead of saying all of the above, given that English was Francesco's third language, I simplified my response. "I had their wines once in New York," I said. "They were unlike any others I have had."

Francesco said, "I hope it will work out. I'll call again tomorrow morning. I talked to that Ribo, he doesn't like to talk to journalists."

"You're kidding me, right?" I asked.

He was not kidding. I knew that the duo was famous for being reclusive and difficult, but I didn't think that reserve would extend to me. I was distraught. Francesco had told Ribo I was a good friend and, not knowing how they felt, said I was an American wine journalist. "Then Ribo asked me what your last name was. Alice, I didn't know what it was! That's when he hung up on me."

"What? He actually hung up on you?"

"That's okay. I don't care. I'll call again tomorrow." He tried again to sound comforting.

The morning was cool and so clear that the hills seemed to be outlined in pencil. I hopped into Francesco's car; we drove north on the west side of the Rhône River. "Tell me," he asked, "how is Miss Knish?"

I caught him up on what I knew about her, which was very little.

"Tell me—Miss Knish, she is in the wine business. Why does she wear perfume? Very bad. I don't understand this."

I had never talked about this with Francesco, but it had been the topic of conversation in New York, especially when Miss Knish was pouring wine. It is infuriating as well as confounding when people in the wine business wear scent. I said, "Miss Knish says she wears essential oil and not perfume."

"What is this essential oil? Is it essential?"

"It's perfume!" I answered, throwing my hands up in the air.

Most people in the wine business learn to live in a scent-free environment because perfumes, scents, those damned house fragrances or scented candles, body lotion, you name it, all interfere with assessing aroma. Once, an Irish novelist came to my house for a social wine tasting. He was reeking of some cologne. At first the Owl Man and I were (uncharacteristically) going to try to ignore it and not say anything. Mr. Irish Novelist was so shy; we thought he would take it morbidly. But when the whole room started to stink and my wines were dwarfed by the smell, action was imperative. Wordlessly, I handed the Owl Man a wet washcloth. He genuflected in front of the Irish Novelist, begged forgiveness, and led the scented one to the sink. The Irish Novelist looked bewildered, and protested, "This isn't cheap stuff." He didn't understand. After all, he was a vodka drinker.

"This is St.-Joseph as well?" I asked Francesco after we had been in the car for fifteen minutes and the landscape had changed dramatically.

Francesco was eager to tell me the history of the area. "There was no St.-Joseph wine before 1956. The area that became the appellation was right where I live in Tournon and Mauves. In 1969, the appellation grew to twenty-five communes from six. There are forty miles of the region. That is too much and a lot of bad wine was made, and there still is. However, St.-Joseph can be a very good wine, very good. But because the appellation is so large and so diluted it has a bad reputation and is hard to sell."

These St.-Josephs are the absolute baddest boys of the Rhône, and my weakness. There is something wilder and more rambunctious about them. From Dard et Ribo, it is their St.-Joseph that I like best. I might even love the Chave St.-Jo over their Hermitage.

By now, Francesco and I were headed to the northernmost part of the Rhône, Chavanay. With many miles in front of us, I had some time to get him talking about his career. After school, he had set up business as a wine-making consultant. He also sources bulk wine and great grapes for winemakers or merchants called *negoçiants*—those who make wine from purchased grapes or wine. This practice is not uncommon, and decades ago was standard in the Rhône and in Burgundy. Now domaines that don't own enough land sometimes buy grapes. Even greats like Chave make wine from purchased fruit. Large-scale winemakers, such as Guigal and Chapoutier, do as well. As a result, Francesco knows just about everything and everyone in the entire north and south appellations, from Chateauneuf-du-Pape to Côte-Rôtie. "When I came here," he explained, "I was the crazy Italian. I was the funny guy working in George the Greek's shop. I studied enology, but winemaking is too . . . introverted. I like to make wine, but I love to talk. I like people, and I need to know, know, know. I love to travel. I need to know and talk about wine. The people here find me very funny. I am not like them. But it was hard. It took a while before they stopped laughing at me and talked to me."

It took ten years before they stopped laughing.

Small towns in France, whose families go back for generations, are famous for always considering inhabitants of foreign origin to be outsiders, however long they have all lived side by side. No matter how excellent George's French is, he will always be "the Greek." Francesco will be the crazy Italian. Francesco's wife, who is from another part of France, has told me that it was difficult even for her to make friends. Erin Cannon Chave, Jean-Louis's American wife, told me she'd had a similar experience. In fact, initially her new surname made her too famous in these parts to actually have friends. People would bow to her on the streets, but never invite her out for a glass of wine. *This hard, stony environment just might make for better wine than people,* I thought. *Hmm*—was this a clue to my relationship with the Owl Man?

"Let's call Jean-Louis for some gossip," Francesco suggested at one point during our drive, pulling out his cell phone.

He got through to Jean-Louis and started to rattle off the names of the winemakers we were visiting that day. When Francesco mentioned Stephane Montez at Domaine du Monteillet, I could hear Jean-Louis shout over the phone. *"Une disastre!"*

Jean-Louis knew me, he had tasted with me. He couldn't understand why I would go to visit such a modernist. I realized *I* had become the gossip! NOTED AMERICAN WINE JOURNALIST WHO CHAMPIONS AUTHENTIC WINES VISITS ONE OF THE RHÔNE'S MOST MODERN STYLISTS.

"Alice said she wanted to go to someone who made a wine like Shiraz," Francesco explained.

"Ah, fine. Yes. I see. Who else?" Jean-Louis asked.

"Dard et Ribo."

I clapped. *Yay.* That bastard Francesco had held out on me.

We arrived at Domaine du Monteillet, a magnificent compound of old, old buildings, which had been in Montez's family for centuries. In 2006, Parker "Parkerized" Montez with his review of the Côte-Rôtie.

> The brilliant, dense plum/purple-tinged 2003 Côte Rôtie Les Grandes Places boasts sweet, floral aromas interwoven with scents of smoked herbs, blackberries, bacon fat, and cassis. This massive, rich, tannic, backward, primary 2003 needs 2–3 more years of bottle age. It should keep for 15 or more years.
>
> —*Wine Advocate* #163 (Feb. 2006) $75

I don't like my Côte-Rôtie "sweet." The purple tinge sounds more typical of Australian Shiraz. I remembered what Jean-Louis had said on the phone: *"Une disastre."* I was walking into this winery with eyebrows raised. When we entered the compound gates, I could not see or smell a Stephane Montez. So we pottered around. The temperature had risen; I looked for shade. After ten minutes, a man in his early thirties emerged from one of the farmhouses. He was shaggily handsome, with an intense air. *"Pardonnez-moi, je faisais soutirage,"* he said, referring to the process known as racking in English, the activity of moving wine from one barrel into another. The purpose of *soutirage* is to oxygenate the wine to relieve the intensity of that musky, skunky Syrah aroma. Some people use the micro-oxygenation technique to get around racking, but Montez still did it the old-fashioned way.

He began our tour. The cold room where the white wines were stored and vinified smelled like a carpenter's workspace, not a winery. After a visit there from his somewhat-loony mom, who reminded me of a great-aunt at a bar mitzvah (Tante Shirley, flashing her beach-happy cleavage), we moved to where he kept the reds.

The usual way to taste is to start with the simplest wine and move up to the more complex. With New World winemakers, this means we start with no oak influence seen on the wines and segue to the most oaked wines. It is not uncommon that as the wines get more "important," I like them less. For our first wine, Stephane picked up a pipette, the glass siphon used to pull wine samples from the cask. He dribbled the sample into my glass. After all of that Parker hype, I was expecting a total Shiraz moment. But the St.-Jo had the agreeable horsey character of Syrah. "They're really not so bad," I whispered to Francesco as Stephane stepped out for a moment. "I mean, they are modern tasting but not *Australia*." Francesco gave me a thin-lipped smile, as if to say, Maybe not, but wait and see what comes next.

And sure enough, tasting the next wine, I noticed a flattened-out aspect. I asked, "Do you cold soak?" This is a common practice of chilling the grape juice down before fermentation to extract color and flavor. This is not necessarily bad, but when done for too long or at excessively cold temperatures, it can freeze out life.

"There is a lot of stuff you can do with temperature," Stephane said, and told me how much he had learned by making wine in

Australia, South Africa, California, even England. He next poured the 2001 Côte-Rôtie—which had spent a whopping thirty-three months in new oak. (Oh, for a taste of the *sans soufre,* Jean-Michel Stephan's Côte-Rôtie, grown on his old vines, with not even a speck of flashy new oak. The wine speaks with the power of a true-blooded, muscular racehorse.) This wine was riddled with espresso-coated, marzipan flavors from the intense wood and who knows what else. I heard Jean-Louis refrain, *"Une disastre,"* and understood. Stephane, not sensing my displeasure, explained, "For me, you have to use heavy toast. I believe in new oak, it brings out the complexity."

There is no accounting for taste. To me this wine was total dreck. When I taste espresso flavors in a wine, I register the flavors as phony and artificial. Oh sure, I know this man was using gorgeous grapes, just like the fellow from Paso Robles. When making a seventy-five-dollar bottle, who doesn't grow grapes well? But Montez was snuffing the life out of the wine. That sort of toasty oak does not age. It does not disappear. It will always leave a cosmetic varnish on the wines.

The only antidote for such an experience? The likes of Dard et Ribo. And so Francesco and I traveled to the other side of the river. Driving to Crozes-Hermitage we passed through l'Tain Hermitage, and I noticed that George the Greek's lovely wine shop was shuttered: dejected and abandoned.

"What happened?" I asked Francesco.

"He closed up. I don't know."

It wasn't surprising, I thought. George poured all of those expensive bottles of Champagne, gave everyone a great time, fed them at nightly parties, and took in no money. How could anyone afford to keep that up? It was Erin Chave who finally filled me in. George had moved back to his other shop, a few blocks away, that his nephew Mikus ran on the Place Taurobole. George the party animal, Erin thought, probably got bored and lonely on the side street where his shop was.

At 2:30, right on time, we arrived at the Dard et Ribo winery in the appellation of Crozes-Hermitage. The sun and heat were full-throttle. The winery looked like a run-down barn in the middle of the Catskills—all sorts of *schmutz* and broken-down farm equipment were strewn around the grounds. Off to the side stood a clutch of old fruit trees. At the door there was a black sign that read DRRRINNNGG! next to the buzzer. I *drrranngg* it but no one answered. The place was like George's shuttered shop, no one home. "We're going to be stood up," I said, feeling forlorn. I puttered about in the blinding sun, looking for shade. "He hates journalists. He hates me."

"He'll come." Francesco assured me. "Don't worry. But it is only Ribo. Rene Dard won't come."

"Why?" I asked, disappointed.

"Just be grateful we have one of them!" he said, jiggling his watch for emphasis. After fifteen minutes, a truck drove up in a cloud of swirling dust. François Ribo stepped out. As he shut the truck door, he mumbled apologies that didn't seem all that sincere. He had a gentle face, wire-framed glasses, and hair that fell in soft blond waves. His black T-shirt celebrated a local film festival. His look screamed counterculture. I found myself filled with questions having nothing to do with wine: what kind of music he listened to and what kind of books he read. But he had allowed us two hours. There wasn't much time to talk about anything except the matter at hand—his wine.

He met all of my questions with grunts of *oui* or *non*. The man—who, in the fictional version of my journey, I would fall in love with, join forces with, and fight an SDS-inspired war against modern wines and the powerful media outlets that foster them—was going to be a huge disappointment. *All right,* I thought, *Picasso was a jerk, too.* I love Philip Roth, but evidently he didn't do too well with women. I resigned myself. *No magical experience here.* He was simply not interested. So I focused on noting the utter mess of the winery (always a good sign to me; nothing worse than a winery as clean as a laboratory) and tasting the wines. Oh, it was the same old boring crap. We barrel tasted the whites, then the reds. Then we tasted out of bottle. Ribo was on total remote control. Even though he didn't like journalists, he knew the program. But I would really rather have sat down, drunk a bottle of wine with him, and talked film.

When we had progressed to tasting from finished bottles, I got up the nerve to ask about taking pictures. Sensing his discomfort, I was hasty, not taking the time I needed to focus. In all of my shots, he came out looking like a fuzzy angel from a Wim Wenders film. I couldn't really believe this angel was an ogre. *Please.*

He couldn't be. So I looked around the dramatically cluttered winery and the former dance therapist within me started to extrapolate on the mess: *creative energy, pot smoking, saxophone player, careful, practical.* His body language wasn't arrogant. He touched his chest a lot, not thumping, but with fingers outstretched over the breastbone, protectively, and at times he giggled. Not laughed but giggled. I decided he was shy. I'm shy as well. That's why I was getting *oui*ed and *non*ed to death, no details. My new understanding helped a little.

Wine questions I can handle in French, so I tried to use my own skill and not rely on Francesco's translation. *"Pourqoui vous ne vendez pas vos vins en Étas Unis?"* I asked, fully knowing that Big Joe had set his mind to import from Dard et Ribo again. But Ribo, who hadn't yet met Joe, and had yet to be persuaded, seemed quite firm. The United States might need his wines, he said, but he did not need the U.S. drinker. He was happy having fanatic Parisian and Japanese drinkers.

Then I asked him, *"Pourquoi vous n'aimez pas journalists?"* This time I got a little bit more of a response.

He said, "It's nice when the critics say nice things, but they can kill you quickly as well." He didn't say anything about Robert Parker. He seemed not to be the least bit interested in the critic's popularity. In fact, he kept referring to his first U.S. importer, a man called Robert Kacher, as "Robert Parker Imports."

I finally decided I had nothing to lose. If we were both shy, we weren't going to get anywhere. Sometime after we tasted the Crozes-Hermitage but before the St.-Joseph, I got very frustrated.

I blurted out, "I love your wines. I am trying to find out something about you. I am trying to find out what it is about you that can make wines this pure and expressive. You're not giving me anything. What music do you listen to? What do you read? What do you drink? Francesco, translate that for me, *please!*"

This was not my most articulate moment. This was not a high point in journalism. This was my one shot, and he was being so confounding! But the ice cracked a little. Ribo started to laugh, or giggle, that *tee-hee* sort of thing. "I have that, too," he said almost empathically, in French I could well understand. "I love wine and want to know the person who made it. I understand."

So I found out that he doesn't read fiction. He reads political history. I still don't know what music he listens to.

"Why don't you like visitors?" I asked. He answered with a touch of newfound intimacy. "If people want to come, they'll come by and knock. They don't have to call. If they feel so strongly, they can just come by. If I hang up on them, they can call back."

What was left of our time together was spent with a new amity. My absolute favorite wine of the day was the St.-Jo, all silk and velvet. Soft tannins melted into the purity of baking bread and smoke and a touch of lime. Everything was in synthetic cork, a sign of contempt for the frivolous. There was no time for nonsense. Surprising me, Francesco bought six bottles of wine to take home. Ribo said good-bye, happy to get rid of the nonfluent American wine writer. In the car, I said, "Well?"

Francesco, nervously jiggling his watch, said, "I'm not used to this kind of wine. It is something else. But it makes me think."

I supposed I could have said something like that about the Owl Man, who also made me think, made me feel. Who forced me into looking at life and the world in a way that was skinned and vulnerable.

- 4 -

Rioja Loses
Its Spanish Accent

My panic about Rioja started when Skinny and I attended Madrid Fusion, a conference that delivers the inside scoop on the latest in avant-garde food techniques and trends. These kinds of events can be fairly tame, but every once in a while there's a new trend that kicks me in the stomach. This time, with a large image of a big fish projected onto the screen behind him, an enthused chef addressed the audience about the use of fish eye, socket, and scale in soups and other dishes. Skinny, who salivates at the mention of a sweet blood pudding, began to think more kindly of vegetarians. She does eat fish eyes, but somehow the idea of squishing them up did her in. She thinks eyes are the way into the soul, even those of a fish.

Leaving Skinny in the fish-eye hall, I fled to the "100 Distinctive Wines of Spain" seminar. I didn't realize I was fleeing from the frying pan into the fire.

I entered a sterile room, classically set up for wine tasting. There were about one hundred settings with ten glasses each. The white-clothed tables faced the dais. Happy to see a familiar face, I plopped myself down next to a cheerful Midwestern pal who really knows his stuff. We fanned through the program to see what was coming. "What the hell is all of this Chardonnay doing here?" he asked me.

Chardonnay is relatively new to Spain. The French grape does its best in a cool climate like that of Burgundy. In hot climates like Spain's, the grape grows fat and sloppy, and almost always needing bags of tartaric acid added to the fermenter to replace what nature hasn't supplied.

"The world does not need a Spanish Chardonnay," I said. My pal nodded in agreement.

"And look, there's no white Rioja!" I added. We shook our heads in mutual disbelief. *Oh, what a world.* We started to taste. Wine after wine, I was disappointed. "These wines don't speak Spanish," I whispered to Doug. "It's as if they went to accent-reducing classes."

It was still the fragile time following the demise of my relationship with the Owl Man, and I was going through a phase where I crumbled when speaking in public. But, forever the whistle-blower, I just had to know, and I hoped I didn't tremble too much. I got the courage to raise my hand. "Why didn't you include any white Rioja in the tasting?" I asked.

The members of the panel didn't have to think too hard about their answer. Ever since Ferran Adria (the brilliant force behind the now-famous restaurant El Bulli) broke the fourth dimension of chefdom by rethinking the character and texture of food, Spain had been at the forefront of the early twenty-first-century avant-garde food movement. Spain was on a roll, and I could almost hear the Spanish wine world saying, "Me, too!" The vignerons wanted attention, and to get it meant scores. They rushed to embrace the modern consumer with modern wine-making styles. Newer wine-growing regions helped the country get recognition. First, it was Priorat that everyone was shouting about. Then came even greater expansion into new wine territory, like Bierzo, Jumilla, Toro, and Montsant. These areas were too new to have wine-growing rules, and land was cheap. The emerging regions offered lower-priced wines that packed a flavor punch. The classics, like old-style Rioja, both red and white, were being discarded and almost seemed stuffy. It seemed as if anything old-fashioned was being shipped to the thrift store with a shrug of "Good riddance."

The moderator replied to my question. "Rioja can't make a good white wine."

Now I was thinking, *Why the hell can't my good-natured pal speak up? Do I always have to be the bad guy?* But I persisted. "Are you saying that the rosé, red, and white wines of Lopez de Heredia are not world treasures? I'm not just saying in Spain, but in the world? Are you actually saying that?"

Lopez de Heredia makes intensely traditional (which happen also to be natural and authentic) wines. Their white might be the last remaining old-style white Rioja in the region. In this case, old-style means long-aged, slightly oxidized wine. It has remarkable (natural) acidity and lively minerality, with threads of fruit and a touch of Brazil nut. In 2007, as is typical for them, their new releases made from the Viura and Malvasia grapes were vintage 1995, 1989, and—get this—1981. In reversal of the normal order, they release the white wines later than the reds. These days, the typical whites released from the region are fresh wines, more typically coming out six months to one year after the vintage. The release of a Lopez de Heredia white is always a love-it-or-hate-it affair. No matter what a drinker's preferences, the wine always gets attention.

When I first visited the Lopez de Heredia winery building, I just adored the look of the place, a nouveau confection with lots of Castilian-lace–like rickrack. If the founder, Rafael Lopez de Heredia, were to walk into the office he would feel nothing had changed despite the passing of 130 years. If he walked into the winery, he would not find any tool or machine he did not know how to use. In fact, I found the winery so untouched by time that it bordered on historical artifact. Most of the other wineries I visited in Rioja had thrown out their old barrels and replaced them with small, new *barriques*. Here, there was hardly a new slat of wood (which do appear when old barrels need repair) in sight. A *tina,* a towering, conical, old oak tank, stood in the dark room like the Oracle. As I took in the sight, the tank started to send out strange sounds—a mystical *slish, slosh,* like the flapping of angels' wings or the rhythm of the ocean. This was the sound of fermentation. Every other winery I had visited had finished but here fermentation stopped when the wine wanted it to, not when the winemaker stopped it.

Maria José Lopez de Heredia, who runs the domaine with her sister Mercedes, also showed me the wine "cemetery," where they kept their older bottles. Think the Addams family's living room. Mold layered the ceiling like insulation. Gook clung to the bottles. Spiders spun their giant webs and scuttled about looking for food. "The spiders are very good, because they eat the insects that can eat the cork," Maria José explained. In the cellars of Lopez de Heredia, the spiders are high tech.

I conjured that whole scene, such a lovely memory for me, as I invoked the name of Lopez de Heredia. But the moderator acted as if I had just called her mother a bag lady. She repeated, "Rioja cannot make great white wine."

Well, hit me over the head with a wet noodle if a gush of support didn't spring forth from the gallery. My support came from the British journalists in attendance, who shared my outrage. The Brits love the old style of white Rioja, a little nutty and oxidative. British-accented argumentative mayhem broke out. The British approved of me. I wasn't alone. Vindication!

The Spanish attempt to reject classic beauty reminded me of the misguided power behind the wrecking ball that demolished New York's Penn Station in the 1960s. It also reminded me of a battle I had once waged with my landlord to preserve my pull-chain toilet, which worked so efficiently. "Lady, this is the twenty-first century, get a real toilet."

It's not that I'm a Luddite for Luddism's sake. Improved technologies, like indoor plumbing and the lightbulb, are good things. But my neighbors who got rid of their toilets? They have constant problems with their plumbing. Me? The pull-chain toilet broke down once in one hundred years. (And I still have the pull-chain model, albeit with some replacement parts.) As a six-year-old, I saw Penn Station the week before it was torn down. Shoulder to shoulder with my fellow second graders, I looked up at the intricate ceiling, openmouthed, and asked, "How can they tear it down?" I burst into tears. "We have to stop it!" I cried. "My father is a lawyer. He can stop it!"

The wines of Lopez de Heredia are the old Penn Stations and pull-chain toilets of the world. There are times when it is pure stupidity to plow forward just to be modern. Because something is modern doesn't mean it is good. But like Penn Station, traditional Rioja (red or white) is going the way of Morse code.

In my early, wine-geek wannabe days, I felt stupid about Rioja. I didn't understand why other people got so excited about it. In either red or white, I found, the wines had a dried-coconut aroma and flavor that reminded me of some grandmotherly perfume I wasn't fond of, something like dried parchment left next to incense. But the real problem with Rioja was me. I had been drinking mediocre bottles that had stayed too long on store shelves, under bad storage conditions. Also, the taste of American oak is spicier than that of French oak, and the long aging of wine in American oak was not familiar to me. Then, when I wasn't looking, a Rioja broke through my defenses. With the Pyrenées as the backdrop, I drank a whisper-soft, twenty-year-old Muga. It made me think of tinned-tomato-juice warmth and was absolutely sunny and delicious. And lurking underneath there was . . . maybe a salty chicken soup with dill and sweet parsnip? I thought, *Yes, now I know the taste of Rioja.* Once I got tuned in to this style, I became hungry for it. It was the wine I chose for Indian food, opting to pair exotic with exotic. I loved it with grilled leeks and any food that had a little smoke. The Rioja system was very handy for the consumer: The wines, historically, were only released when ready to drink; the wineries did the aging. How lovely! A *crianza* was a wine that had two years of age, *reserva* three years, and *gran reserva* at least five years, often much longer.

Wouldn't you know, just as I fell in love with that style of Rioja, it was snuffed out. Old-style Rioja got a bad rap. It's kind of a boring story. The same thing happened with Chianti in Tuscany and Malbec in Argentina. Students returning from wine school used the new techniques that they believed were superior to their grandfathers'. Winemakers who didn't trust themselves hired wine consultants to measure the chemistry of a wine. Retired CEOs hired consultants to create status-symbol wines. Winemakers wanted Parker's attention—and there went the neighborhood. The detractors of the old style said what I had originally thought, that Riojas were too dried out, lacked fruit and freshness, and were too oaky. (Little did they know what truly too oaky tasted like.) They wanted wines that tasted new. Rioja started to lose ground to the more nubile growing regions. Rioja growers responded.

All right now, maybe in the past there weren't enough great Riojas made, but there were certainly *some* greats. Why didn't the new Rioja winemakers look to the greats in the region as their model? Why didn't they emulate the luscious wines of Lopez, Muga, Cune, and La Rioja Alta? Instead, the vintners instituted a solution that was even more expensive than decreasing grape yields and committing to better winemaking. They bought new and smaller barrels to give the wine more wood contact. They went crazy with temperature control, replanted with clones instead of propagating from their own vines, and started using yeasts, enzymes, and, often, machines. The changes turned the once-elegant wine into a denser, chewier one that rarely surprised. During a recent visit I heard quite a few winemakers talk of the way they used micro-oxygenation—such as at the winery Lan—which turned some wines into something like a ganache-covered malt ball, dense on the outside and a cloud on the inside. Slowly, even the holdouts—the wineries I mentioned above (save for Lopez de Heredia)—started to add more modern wines to their output.

I left that tasting at Madrid Fusion saddened. I'd had no idea the situation was so bad.

That night, Skinny and I went to a postconference party. We tasted some newfangled foods (watching out, to avoid any fish-eye or fish-scale additive), such as Ferrán Adrià's parmesan ice cream. *Yum,* I thought. *When new is good, it's good.* There were no wines being served that we could drink, so we sipped some of Adria's experimental cocktails—like his Hot Frozen Gin Fizz, made with lemon juice, simple syrup, and gin, frozen and topped with hot lemon foam. Avant-garde experimentation works way better for me in cocktail and ice-cream culture than with wine.

I returned to New York with my heart in my mouth. I wondered: Could I put on a Supergirl costume and fly over to Rioja, rip out their small, new barrels and micro-oxidation bubblers and throw out their bags of enzymes and yeasts?

The airport taxi dropped me off in front of my building on a globally warmed January day. I looked up the long flight of steps in front of me. Just a year before, the Owl Man would have bounded down and then up those steps, gallantly carrying my load. This time, I schlepped my own bags. Instead of welcome-home flowers or chocolates, a mini-skyscraper of wine samples had piled up in front of my door. Most of the wines—like those from E & J Gallo—came unbidden. Unlike normal people, I find this free wine a nuisance, because most of them are dreadful, not the sort that I write about or even want to taste. Despite frequent calls to publicists, it's been impossible to get off of the sampling lists. About 90 percent of the wines get redistributed to my neighbors, who are very happy for the castoffs.

After going through the mail, e-mail, and phone messages, unpacking, and settling in, I got to the boxes. While taking inventory, deciding which wines stayed, I rescued a Marqués de

Caceres, 1996 Rioja reserva. *How timely!* I pulled the cork, chugged, swirled, spit, and ran to my computer to blog. "If you're looking for a wine with absolutely no sense of place, rush out to buy Marqués de Caceres. Under its cherry vanilla is tannic juice—tannin from wood; I felt my mouth was full of cherry-flavored splinters." I threw the wine out. But that awful experience got me thinking: *What does Mr. Parker think about Rioja?*

I combed *Parker's Wine Buyer's Guide* to search for his favorite Riojas. Winning "excellent" (i.e., cult status) with ratings of 94 and 95 were the Riojas from Bodegas Fernando Remirez de Ganuza. The wine was definitely a Rioja, but Parker's note sounded as if it described a Napa cabernet: "[It] exhibits a sweet, intense nose of melted licorice, road tar, truffles, black currants, cherries, and hints of smoky, toasty oak."

I then went to the Parker competitor, *Wine Spectator.* The top editor at the magazine, Tom Matthews, used to love old-style wines and has always been a soft touch for Spain's. In years past, he's given lots of attention to the Lopez de Heredia wines, but more recently he has become enamored of the newer, bolder, more concentrated style. I contacted him to find out why he now champions the more modern, especially the wines referred to as *vinos de alta expressión,* wines that are not *reserva* or *gran reserva* but something else—the wineries' "special" wines. He wrote back to inform me that, while I could not publish any part of our conversation, he could not stop me from drawing my own conclusions from his writings in the magazine. Fair enough.

In the December 15, 2005, issue of *Wine Spectator,* Matthews wrote of these new wines:

> They display concentrated, ripe fruit flavors, massive structure and lavish oak. Many are single-vineyard bottlings, most are matured in new French oak and few are aged in bottle before release. In other words, they abandon many of Rioja's traditional approaches. This has caused a backlash among some critics, who accuse the wines of being too international in style, of losing a specific and authentic Rioja identity.

I noted that, when he mentioned Lopez de Heredia in his pieces, he often disparagingly wrote, "for a traditional wine." In the December 15, 2005, article he went one further, stating, "In my opinion, the traditional approach [to winemaking] obscured the true character of *terroir* because yields were too high, most wines were blended from many vineyards, and long aging in American oak overshadowed the flavors of the fruit."

So even smart guys like Matthews were looking at those new-fangled producers as an example of how to do it. Why? Was it advertising driven, or were they prey to the pitfall so many face when tasting thousands of wines a year: It's the bigger wines that get noticed. It's the wines that have bling, have flash, that are screaming in front of the class, hands dancing in the air and shouting, "Choose me!" What about the great producers who made a Burgundy-weight Rioja packed with nuance and life and deliciousness? I remember the days when Tom Matthews stood up in a roomful of people and said how sad it was that the taste of place in wine was disappearing. But now place didn't seem to hold any significance for him. Robert Parker keeps his nose clean by not taking advertising. How clean the *Wine Spectator's* nose is has been debatable. In the end, though, it didn't matter why they had turned. Neither was championing authentic, naturally made, elegant wines from Rioja, or from Spain even. I couldn't save Penn Station, but perhaps I could have some effect elsewhere. I needed to see for myself whether Lopez de Heredia was in danger. I needed to find out just how bad the situation was.

ON THE FLIGHT to Bilbao, I begged my way into a bulkhead seat. Being the kind of person brought up to feel guilt with no provocation, I looked uncomfortably at a long-legged football player type crammed into a tiny seat while all five feet and one hundred pounds of me luxuriated in the extra room. Once I overcame an urge to offer a seat swap, though, I indulged in a rare moment of tranquility, happy to be tiny. This trip was before liquids were banned on planes and it was still possible to sneak wine on board disguised as fruit juice in a water bottle. I had some wonderful Gamay from the Loire, which I drank happily. I was just ready to reach for the Ambien when I realized my sleeping potion was in my checked luggage. At the same moment, the infant next to me started to wail. So I read through the night, including an interview with Pedro Lopez de Heredia, Maria José's father. He was quoted as saying, "If we allowed ourselves to be guided by the financial profit that drives many winemakers to use accelerating techniques during the wine making process, our products would lose their personalities."

Wow, I thought, *now there's a father for you.* We don't get to choose our fathers, but Pedro's passion for wine honesty and integrity is what I look for, whether choosing literature, wine, or love.

I was staggeringly tired when I landed in the spring-bright sun, and I slept soundly during the one-hour drive from Bilbao to Haro, where I awoke to the sight of the old Tempranillo vines just coming to life. The fresh leaves pushing from splintery stumps looked like hands reaching for the sun. The silver-tipped Cantabrian Mountains lit up the background. The sandy soil looked like crushed coral. I felt I was standing in the basin of a drained-out sea. Perhaps that's why I found a sea-like savory salinity in so many older Riojan wines.

Haro was the town that put Rioja on the map. Problems in the French vineyards helped make the region famous. In 1849, when a powdery mildew destroyed vineyards, Bordeaux merchants crossed into Rioja and set up consultancies to help Rioja make wine suitable for the French palate. Again, in 1877, when the louse phylloxera ate up their vines' roots, the French looked to the Tempranillo-based wines of Rioja to replace their Bordeaux. So the region has a long history of French influence. The French focused on Haro because it was conveniently located near both Bordeaux and Rioja and directly linked by rail to the ocean for shipping. The town became home to several great wineries, including Muga, Cune, La Rioja Alta, and Lopez de Heredia. All but LdH have added the modern amenities of stainless-steel tanks, new oak, and perhaps a few more tricks as well. The other three are widely thought of as also producing some traditional wines. But, though not wildly modern in their techniques, Cune and Muga do produce some hormonal, over-the-top wines to compete in the *vinos de alta expressión* market. The real old-fashioned cheese—Lopez de Heredia—stands alone.

I was signing in at the hotel when Maria José Lopez de Heredia breezed in to fetch me for lunch. She was ablaze in canary colors: gold eye shadow, lemon-yellow silk scarf trailing behind her Isadora Duncan–style, buttery-looking boots, and a tan corduroy skirt. "Ahlyce!" she cried. "Eeet's goude to zee you ah-gayn! Look at this weather! Eeez gorgeous, no?" She summoned me in her raspy, chirpy voice. "Queeck, we have to run for lunch."

There was a magical, elfin quality to her. If I didn't know she was almost forty, or see the stray silver strand in her head of glossy black hair, I would swear she was sixteen. She was so incredibly cute that I wanted to pinch her cheek, pick her up, and put her in my pocket. I could easily imagine her as a chatterbox child who never stopped to inhale. She was so perky that she woke me right up from my jet-lagged stupor. We ran, sprinted, dashed for the restaurant with such urgency that our lunch might have been the reason that I'd crossed the Atlantic. At home, I hate lunch. I never like taking the time, or spending the calories, and if wine is involved—an occupational hazard—I can never go back to work without a nap. But lunch is an important part of European life, and in Spain it is absolutely sacred. There was no way to avoid it. We slid into a tapas place, Altamauri Restaurante, just seconds before closing time.

The owner turned ashen when he found out I didn't eat meat. In a country where the pig is considered a vegetable, this is problematic. These are the times I need my pig-loving friend Skinny. Her passion for pork is so attention getting that people don't notice I'm pushing the food around on my plate, reaching for the cheese instead. Sweating nervously into his huge mustache, the chef murmured an unconvincing, "No problem," and disappeared into his kitchen. Maria José ordered wine while I noted two women on the stools to our left lighting up cigarettes in front of the NO SMOKING sign. The chef returned, proudly bearing way too many plates of tapas, in hormonal proportions. These are not the dainty tapas of Barcelona, these are the huge, *pinxto*-sized plates of the Basque. The *minestra*—overcooked vegetable stew— had some ham in it (remember, pig is a vegetable), but there was also a salad and a battered piece of Swiss chard draped with a thick potato slice. I was happy to trust that this food was far from avant-garde, that there were no fish scales or eyes in anything. Maria José tittered about me eating like a bird while she packed away lunch with gusto. If I ate like she did, I would turn into a cow, but she, in constant motion, must have the metabolism of a hummingbird. No matter: The star of the show was the 1997 white from her Gravonia vineyard. We had no trouble polishing it off and wanting more, even if there was no nap in my future.

Trained as a winemaker, Maria José is her family's charismatic ambassador to the world. I don't understand how she remains single. How could a woman prone to saying things like, "After a hailstorm, when vines are damaged, you mourn for your vines as if they were children" and "If you have this relationship to the earth, you make a very different wine" not have a trail of suitors?

She must. Suitors, however, would have to compete with the other loves in her life, like her father, Pedro, and the family wine. "My father wanted me to study chemistry," she told me. "That was a big fight in the family, because my grandfather yelled, 'She'll learn how to make wines with no grapes!' I need chemistry. I need to know what to do if something should go wrong. But in modern wine school, when everything is right you are taught it is wrong!"

She went on to tell me that any time the malolactic fermentation commences before alcoholic (the reverse order of things, but often a result of the year's weather patterns), "A UC Davis graduate would drop dead on the spot." Another lesson she didn't listen to at school was to plant clones instead of replanting from their own cuttings, known in French as *selection massale*. The supposedly virus-free clones are developed in the lab and raised in the sterile environment of a nursery. They can never produce grapes with the complexity that vineyard selection can. Bred for certain flavors, bred to produce grapes that are more precocious than those grown under *selection massale,* they are viewed as an economic boon and a safer choice. I often get press releases in which a winery proclaims the careful selection of clones for their vineyard, but Maria José says, "We will never use them. You need three hundred clones from a nursery to give the complexity of one real vine."

"I met Mr. Parker once," she volunteered. "When I told Pedro," she said, referring to her father, "that I was going to have lunch with him, he told me I could only go if he promised not to write about the wine. Pedro explained, 'Because if he writes about our wines, we won't have any to sell!'" She found Parker charming. "I have no problem with him," she said. "He loves our wine."

I wasn't going to be the one to break it to her that she and her *padre* were delusional. Parker told me that Rioja is overrated and, as far as the LdH white Rioja is concerned, "I hate those wines. I won't review them because I don't need any more enemies." He likes the reds enough but, he said, "I like their neighbor, La Rioja Alta, better."

In June 2005, Parker reviewed two LdH red wines, from the Tondonia and Bosconia vineyards. He ranked them 87 and 90. He called the color on the 1987 Tondonia "feeble." He said the wine had "early maturity," meaning it got old before its time. The wine he tasted was nearly twenty years old. It had earned its lovely color. No one would expect it to be dark and dense. It deserved some gray hairs. As wine ages and evolves, with the gradual effect of oxygen, the flavors evolve (the fruit fades, the tannins sweeten) and the colors change. White wines get darker, becoming amberish, and red wines turn to brick. When I taste a wine, especially in a blind tasting, I count on its color to tell me both its age and its grape varietal. A dark color for a twenty-year-old wine would have been thoroughly unnatural.

Most people are not like the Lopez de Heredias, who have such conviction in the wine they make that they can shrug off "feeble" coming from a wine reviewer. Most would hire the next-available Bordeaux wine consultant to change their wine so that no one could call it names. Arguably, comments like this one paved the way for traditional houses, like fellow Haro winery Cune, to make wines more like Bordeaux and less like the classic Rioja wine with its "feeble" color. These are wines made not out of love, but fear, fear that Parker will scold the winemakers with his epithets. Thus the color obsession of people like Fernando Remirez de Ganuza—a producer prized by Parker—was born. In fact, this same color obsession prompted Barolo makers in Piedmont to add cabernet illegally to their Nebbiolo (to give the naturally garnet-colored wine a purple haze) and made winemakers worldwide start adding powdered tannins and enzymes (to try to glue a color in place, no matter what color the grape naturally wants to produce).

When I met Fernando (so loved by Robert Parker), he was such a sweetheart, with his polished hair, pigskin jacket, and gentlemanly ways. I wanted to like his wines. A quick look around his antiseptic winery recast my expectations in line with reality. We stopped in front of a new fermentation tank (he changes not only his barrels every year, but also fermentation tanks), and he began to talk about how hard he works on color. He didn't talk about flavor—but color. I knew then that he would pull every trick he could to pump it up. No surprise that when I asked Fernando if he uses enzymes for color, he said of course he does. When I asked him why color was important, he not only mentioned Robert Parker but said that color was indicative of a great wine.

Well, deliver me from brawn and give me feeble. Deliver me from wines like Fernando's and give me the Lopez de Heredias with their intense delicacy. When Lopez de Heredia buckles—if ever—that style of wine is gone and cannot be replaced. I asked Maria José, "Are you sad about the way things are going right now in Rioja?" Her answer shocked me.

"Wine has been worse in Rioja. It's not so bad now. There are good wines being made, but we are 'the last of the Mohicans,'" she said, with tremendous pride. She actually liked being the last one.

That puzzled me, but it also reminded me of some elderly people I have known who, once they turned ninety-five, felt a certain pride for having lasted so long.

That night, it rained with a biblical flood–like vengeance. Bone soaked and exhausted from visiting four wineries, I collapsed in the hotel room, then collapsed again into a chair at their restaurant, where I ordered a half bottle of the basic Cune wine. While I waited for its arrival, I wrote up my thoughts from the day. I was satisfied that Lopez de Heredia would survive at least through my lifetime. Unfortunately, I did not see much hope of the current crop of wineries reclaiming the old style of winemaking. Many had retired their old barrels—and those old American oak barrels

are a big part of the historical picture. Almost all had become be-
lievers in micro-oxygenation, and several were hopping on the
reverse-osmosis bandwagon. But more importantly, to make wine
in the old way means the wine must take its time—and current
economics preclude newcomers' taking up to eight years to release a wine, as is needed with many of the *gran reservas*. There
might, though, be a hint of greater awareness about natural
winemaking techniques, despite the love affair with better-
manipulation-through-chemistry that had entrapped so many
wineries in the region. Ironically, the seed of future hope might
be with a Frenchman, Olivier Rivière. I never met him in Spain
but rather in France, on the hardcore natural-wine circuit. Olivier
is one of the only local winemakers who holds up Lopez de Heredia as the Example. He himself uses smaller barrels and yes, they
are French. He works with what nature gives him. It is still quite
early in his career, but he is a winemaker to watch, for sure.

I was enjoying my Cune. It was the 2000, before the wine had
changed. It was drinkable, but it was no Lopez de Heredia. I
scouted the menu for something I could eat. There was my Spain
standby, tinned white asparagus. It's a wine-and-food match that
would send a sommelier out to me with a red marker. I enjoyed
being alone and fully experiencing this moment, eating tinned asparagus, not having to apologize for not eating flesh or for making this un-classic wine pairing. My fork piercing the mushy
asparagus, I overheard British-accented English. In front of me sat
two sixtyish gentlemen, one with Dickensian, long gray hair. Not
shy about eavesdropping, I determined that they had bought cheap

Ryanair tickets in the 99-pence fall sale and come here to hike in the Cantabrian Mountains. After hearing about their washout of a day, I heard the tale of a friend of theirs who, though a problematic alcoholic, had been a great composer. Just after he died from drink and poverty, his music sold like hotcakes. But the arrangements transformed the music into something their friend would never have approved of. I couldn't help myself from breaking into their conversation. "I'm sorry for listening in," I said, "but that is one of the saddest stories I've ever heard." Thinking of my own struggles with the writing life, I felt a connection to the tale. I also saw broader associations. "You know," I said, "your story is also a metaphor for the demise of Rioja just at the moment when it can be great. When the world is ready for it, it has disappeared."

I noticed that they had not even attempted to finish a bottle of wine from Ostatu, the Gloria to be exact. In the April 2004 issue of *The Wine Advocate,* Robert Parker rated it 94:

2001 Gloria de Ostatu (95% Tempranillo from 60–70 year old vines and 5% Graciano) was aged 18 months in new French oak, and bottled unfiltered. This fabulous effort offers a saturated ruby/purple color as well as gorgeous aromas of cigar tobacco, smoke, black currants, blackberries, and cedar. Deep, full-bodied, and opulent, with a voluptuous mid-section, great intensity, and fine purity, this is a superb offering. Sadly, only 500 cases were produced. Drink it over the next 10–15 years. This is clearly a winery of which to take note, and the influence of the brilliant Hubert de Bouard can not be discounted.

Out of curiosity I asked my fellow diners what they thought of it.

"We can't drink it," Mr. Dickens said.

I wasn't surprised. Ostatu was one of the wineries I had visited, and I thought the wines tasted more like California Merlot taking a stab at being Bordeaux. It was a prime example of the so-called progress in the region. The winemakers had told me, with some pride, that one day, Bordeaux consultants knocked on their door and complimented their gorgeous vineyards, and the next thing they knew they were in collaboration, making wines that the *Wine Spectator* and Parker liked. I thought that their wine needed identity counseling.

I urged the Dickensian gentlemen to get the Cune *crianza,* the safest and cheapest wine on the list.

The next day I was off to Bilbao, to end my trip where it began. Skinny arrived from San Sebastian to meet me. "Did you have anything good to drink?" I asked.

"No!" she yelled.

Then I unburdened myself. "The situation in Rioja is worse than I thought, Skinny. There are a lot of new players, but almost everyone is making a wine in a completely different style now. The wines come in one size, extra large. Delicate, gorgeous, elegant, perfumed, chicken soup and dill—it's all gone."

Yet we were determined to drink something really good as we greedily remembered that bargain of an old Rioja we'd had in the Pyrenées. Maybe we wouldn't find any Lopez de Heredia, but maybe some older La Rioja Altas? Maybe even from before the winery started to use new oak?

We set off to our dinner spot, which was not at all charming—in fact, it was as bright as a dentist's office. It was popular, though. We fought our way past the tight-jean crowd to a standing-room place at the bar. The owner, who attempted to take care of us, spoke only Basque and Spanish. We spoke neither. I handed over my card. He didn't speak English but he did understand the phrase, *wine writer.* "Journalist?" he asked.

I wrote out a little wish list of wines we were interested in. This guy owns a wine bar, I thought, so surely when he sees Lopez de Heredia at the top of the list, he'll know what we're after. But he shook his head as if my list was a foreign language. So I expanded it to include wines I could tolerate even in newer vintages: Cune, La Rioja Alta, Marqués de Riscal, and Muga. Now I was absolutely convinced that this would clue him in that we wanted authentic Rioja, a wine with under 13 percent alcohol, a blend of three local red grapes—Tempranillo, Mazuelo, and Graciana—medium-brick color, aged in a fairly old American oak barrel of about 600 ml. A wine with delicacy and complexity.

He scratched his head as if he didn't have a clue what those wines were. I felt like I had walked up to some pierced hip-hop DJ and asked for Charles Trenet. The man looked befuddled: I was supposed to be a wine writer, so what was I doing with that list of old farts? He showed us some other bottles. He tried to tempt us with those newfangled wines that Tom Matthews likes so much. I shook my head no. Then he remembered that there was a Muga after all. He emerged with the Aro, which, of course, is one of those expensive (120 dollars in the States), overoaked wines, *vinos de alta expressións*. I flipped through my tasting notes and read, *Oak-coated Concord grape*. Forget it.

I made the sign of the cross, as if heading off a vampire. He must have thought I was crazy; this 2001 Aro had been given 98 points by Parker! He wrote:

An inky/purple color is accompanied by sumptuous aromas of lead pencil shavings, creme de cassis, incense, black tea, flowers, and sweet cherries. Opulent and full-bodied, with high levels of tannin, and wonderful sweetness as well as definition, it is a tour de force in winemaking.

I looked around. The Bilboans were ordering bottle after heavy bottle of modern wine. "My father's a lawyer," I said to Skinny. "He can stop this."

"Your father died last year; he's out of business," she said to me. I realized that my dad, being the kind of guy who could drink anything, wouldn't have helped. Anyway, these crimes against wine, like knocking down Penn Station, are perfectly legal.

Our helpful master of ceremonies finally came up with a wine from Cune called Imperial in a new vintage. Okay. We could put up with it. I nodded, affirmative. We smiled politely, and he went to get it for us. As we were being set up with glasses, we eyed the tapas list. The most appealing one was a huge sliced pickle doused with chopped onions and that preserved tuna that the Spanish do so well in vinaigrette. We pointed to it on the menu. The waiter, clad in pumpkin-colored pants, nodded to us. He poured the wine and set off to get us food. Skinny took a great, big gulp of the wine and then frowned. I sniffed it. *Damn.* It was corked—smelled like a moldy basement. We didn't know how to say "corked" in Spanish. Getting the owner's attention, I pinched my nose and then pointed to the bottle. The owner quickly whisked it away and produced a fresh bottle. With trepidation, I smelled it. It was corked again! This time I wanted to put Skinny up to the task. She is younger and skinnier than I am and knows how to use it to advantage. But she couldn't do it. "Maybe he'll just notice that we aren't drinking it," she said, like a wimp. Feeling like a complete loser, I caught the man's attention, shrugged my shoulders, pointed to the bottle, and shook my head mournfully. The crowd was heating up, like it was the only *pinxto* place in town. (Out of about a million *pinxto* places in Bilbao . . .) With a look that made me feel like the biggest pain in the ass, our man came over and this time, he smelled it. He took the bottle away, soon to return with a new one. His eyes took on a twinkle, a smile stretched from ear to ear. He was so pleased with himself. In English, he said to us, "The best in Rioja."

The wine was a 2000 Remirez de Ganuza, a wine from that sweet-natured control freak obsessed with color. I had already tasted this—albeit a newer vintage. Skinny hadn't. We gave in. The wine was poured. The owner looked on approvingly, I toasted the owner, and we sipped.

"We can't win," I said to Skinny. "We just can't win."

– 5 –

Who Stole the Krug?

The day the Towers fell, my very close friends gathered on the rooftop of my tenement apartment, about a mile north of the devastation. We were close enough to feel the grit and smell the smoke, yet the direction of the wind kept us from being showered with debris. With us was a friend who worked for the Clicquot Champagne company. Thinking this might be the end of the world, and allowing for the possibility that this would be our last opportunity to drink whatever great wines we had lying about, she had brought over a few bottles of La Grande Dame rosé, Clicquot's prestige cuvée, which retails for about 150 dollars. We drank them while breathing the toxic purple smoke still blowing from the site we couldn't rip our gaze from. The irony of drinking Champagne—traditionally a celebratory wine—at such a time was not lost on us. In a while the bottles were gone, and I scrounged around for something more for us to drink on this last day on earth. I tried to choose bottles bearing in mind our possible doom. *Why save the good stuff?* I started to pick out the bottles that I wanted to drink up in case I had to evacuate. The first bottle, a Sagrantino, tasted like sawdust; another Burgundy tasted like mud. It didn't take a genius to see that sorrow had soured our taste buds. We collectively decided that nothing would taste great that night, so we stuck with bubbles, to paraphrase Madame Lily Bollinger: good in pain and great in joy.

It was difficult not to recall this night when I was asked to travel to Champagne a few years later. The magazine wanted a story on the trend toward bottling single-vineyard Champagnes, or as they call them in the region, mono cru Champagne. I had occasionally passed by the region but never had a reason to immerse myself in the land of bubbles. I casually mentioned my upcoming trip to my old Boston roommate, Honey-Sugar, to which she replied, "I have no idea what the hell single-vineyard Champagnes are."

I explained that, historically, Champagne is made from a blend of the grapes culled from the greater region. Grapes for mono cru Champagne come from one, specific vineyard that has some demonstrated greatness. The most famous of these are Krug's all-Chardonnay Clos de Mesnil and Philliponat's Clos des Goisses. Mono crus are unusual because blend is the nature of Champagne.

"But why do they blend from all over?" asked Honey-Sugar. "Champagne's rather large, no?"

Because the weather stinks, I told her. At least it did pre–global warming. In 2003, the grapes got so ripe that most Champagne houses could have made normal wine, but usually, the grapes that are used in Champagne, Pinot Noir, Pinot Meunier, and Chardonnay, just don't ever get ripe enough—acidity is off the charts. It's painful to taste the still wines. Once, at Krug, I tasted through about thirty samples in a blending exercise. Afterward, I felt I needed both a gastroenterologist and a dentist. But blending and bubbles can hide a multitude of sins. Making Champagne is like making lemonade out of lemons. And the finely honed ability of each house's blender to achieve a consistent blend became a source of regional pride. So blending not only became the norm, it became tradition. Tradition is God in France. To mess with tradition there is blasphemy.

Honey-Sugar was uncommonly silent throughout my little lecture.

"Are you with me, Honey-Sugar?" I asked. "Should I stop?"

"Go on," she said.

Not needing much encouragement, I hopped right back on my soapbox. I told her how Champagne is dominated by the big houses known as Grandes Marqués (basically big labels) and the biggest of these have been gobbled up by global companies. Moët Hennessy Louis Vuitton owns the most famous Grandes Marqués in Champagne—Moët, Veuve Cliquot, Krug, and the lesser-known Mercier and Ruinart. Though LVMH is a large landowner, the company still doesn't grow enough for its needs. Like almost all big houses, LVMH depends on grapes from the local farmers—the growers.

"I still don't get why this mono cru is a big deal," said Honey-Sugar. "Yes, it is tradition. But it has to be more than that, no?" she astutely pointed out.

"Ah, of course. This is a situation where the little guy is threatening the big corporations."

"Let's hear it for the little guy. *Yay!* But how?"

I went on with my lecture, telling her how some of the independent landowners/growers started to save fruit for themselves in order to make small-batch Champers. People started to call them "grower Champagnes." Industrial and chemical farming is prevalent in Champagne. But the best of the small growers sweat over their land, pamper the soil as if their vineyards were grand cru Burgundy, go as organic as they can, and create wines with loads of character. The wine geeks went crazy for them. Of course, Clicquot and Möet didn't lose market share—for every drinker who wants a grower Champagne there are a thousand who want their Champagne to have a recognizable label, be a brand. As the marketing director of Clicquot told me, selling face cream or Champagne is the same thing, a little product and a lot of dream. Yet there also started to exist a kind of wine lover who would never buy a Grande Marqué, because they want all product. So the suspicion is not so much that Möet wanted to make a mono cru, but wanted to add a kind of wine that might appeal to the Champagne-drinking wine geek. It's a little like Hershey's trying to get into the artisanal-chocolate market, I explained. Same thing.

Though I was convinced I was boring her, Honey-Sugar must have been hanging on every word, because a few days later she called to tell me that her husband had given his blessing, and a plane ticket. She was coming with me. "Al," she said, "this will be our girl trip, like twenty years ago!"

I was in a difficult place. I was looking forward to my solo adventure, in part to revisit my youth, to contemplate life and love. I wanted to be morose if I felt like it, I wanted to have affairs if they came along. I didn't think I wanted company. What's more, in the past my dear friend hadn't been able to calibrate her Southern charm, which had often embarrassed me. And I know very well that my work doesn't look like work from the outside, but have no doubt: It is indeed work. Some who have tried to tag along on my European sorties have been felled by the tasting pace, starting at eight in the morning and continuing until the wee hours. There's tromping in the vines regardless of weather. There are bone-chilling cellars and endless conversations about fermentation and pruning techniques, which might cause Honey-Sugar's eyes to glaze over. Dinners often end way past midnight, and then we're off early in the morning to start another day of appointments. Factor in the jet lag, and it all could equal a sort of hell.

I warned her, but she was not put off. "You know I love Champagne," she said. "We'll have a great time."

But just to be sure, I had one of those difficult conversations— about her decibel level. I asked her to be as quiet as she had been when I was describing the mono cru. "I won't open my mouth," she said. "Promise, Al." A few weeks later, we were headed toward La Champagne.

No matter what the season, when riding through the twisty roads of Champagne I've always been struck by how corporate, manicured, and sterile the vineyards look. And in the summer, when the green vines contrast with the pure, white soil like stripes on a school-green chalkboard, the sense of sterility is most striking. The huge vines are immaculately shaped, as if cut from a template.

Our first stop was Moët Chandon, the Champagne giant. In 2001, this now thirty-six-million-bottle gorilla debuted three different Champagnes—each made entirely from a single grape variety grown in a single vineyard. One from Chardonnay, one from Pinot Noir, and one from Pinot Meunier. The trio was packaged as La Trilogie de Grands Crus, with a retail price of 275 dollars. Almost instantly upon its release, other mono cru Champagnes bubbled up on wine-store shelves, mostly from merchants like Nicholas Feuillatte and Mailly. This minibubble of mono cru was a microfad, it seemed, one I doubted would go anywhere.

I had to ask why an international giant like Moët was trying to enter the small market carved out by niche, artisanal producers. After all, the small guys represent a mere 2+ percent of producers in the Champagne business. Surely, Moët sells enough wine. How could this megaproducer feel threatened?

There was a nasty rain falling when Honey-Sugar and I squirreled out of our small car in Moët's Epernay parking lot, where a statue of Dom Perignon loomed, seeming to bless headquarters and the lucrative public tasting room. Inside, the building was very corporate and hushed—not surprisingly, given those manicured stripes of vines that lined Champagne's covered hills. Women walked around in Kenzo designer shawls, available in the gift shop. Honey-Sugar tugged at my jacket. "I want one of those! Do you think they'll give us one?" I kicked her.

We met Georges Blanck, Moët's dapper head winemaker, and after the initial niceties and polite jokes about the weather, we were off to see the vineyards. First stop was the grand-cru village of Aÿ, planted with one of the three Champagne grapes, Pinot Noir. We froze our tootsies off. Dressed for a cool day in July, I did have a jean jacket, which I desperately clutched to myself. Honey-Sugar was less fortunate, as her jacket had been pinched at JFK. I gave her my shawl (not Kenzo), but within seconds we were being pelted by icy rain and shivering in forty-degree weather, utterly miserable. With a whisper to me—"Okay. I get what you meant about the weather"—my friend retreated to the car while I risked pneumonia and poked about the vineyard asking questions. Blanck apologized, as if the weather were his fault. He talked about the beauty of the vineyard soil, about the supremacy of the chalk. He talked about the constant threat of erosion.

Cold and shaking among Moët's Pinot Noir vines in Aÿ, I wasn't convinced that it was a beautiful vineyard, nor was I convinced that Moët cared how to work it. In fact, the famed chalky-white soil wasn't "worked" at all—it looked dead, with a cadaverlike grayness. Chemical weed killers had clearly been deployed instead of vineyard plows. *No wonder erosion is of constant concern,* I thought, *there's nothing growing here to keep the soil in place.*

Scattered about were bits of robin's-egg-blue plastic, evidence of the notorious "fertilizer" made from recycled toxic trash that a Paris company sold to vineyards until 1998, shockingly still to be found despite the passing of several years. Some vineyards look and smell so delicious that they make me want to speed home to crack open a bottle. To put it delicately, Le Sarments d'Aÿ, and many of the others I saw in Champagne, are not among them.

After another muddy, sodden trip to another vineyard, this one planted with Chardonnay, we finally went back to the ranch to thaw out and taste through the wines. M. Blanck and his marketing manager ushered us into a sleekly designed room, replete with bits of chintz mixed with Deco streamlining. M. Blanck, his double-breasted suit jacket arranged just so, looked at my fingers, which had lost all color, and again apologized for the weather. I said, "It wouldn't be Champagne if the weather were predictable."

"Hah," he laughed politely. He fluffed his white breast-pocket kerchief. The nails of his hands were clean and clipped, unlike the hands of most winemakers I knew. Honey-Sugar sat next to me, being very good about keeping her charm in check. She looked forward to her first glass of Champagne of the trip. I was less eager. I had tasted the Trilogie wines at a press event a few years back and was unimpressed. But I needed to be fair and keep my prejudice in check.

We started with the Chardonnay, the Vignes de Saran. I found it floury and dusty, a bit like mushroom powder with a touch of honey. Yet there was a nice lingering acidity. The all-Pinot-Meunier Sillery won my kindest notes: an appealing rosy smell, with a bit of limeade. Then there was the Pinot Noir, from the Aÿ vineyard, which produced a wine with an unmistakable Breyers vanilla-ice-cream quality. Blanck went on at length about the differences in the soil of each vineyard and how the wines exhibited these distinct qualities.

I asked Blanck if they were really trying to show the differences in their wines, why not use the grapes' own indigenous yeasts?

He went prickly on me. Being a controlled sort of man, however, he did not raise his voice, he just got ever-so-slightly tremulous. "Sometimes it gets me angry, this question about yeasts," he said.

Still, I pushed anyway. "When you use commercial yeasts to control the fermentation and flavors of the wine, how can you say that you are expressing the *terroir*?"

As if it were an explanation, he told me that they had used signature yeast developed in their labs from their own grapes. And, anyway, it was impossible, "utterly impossible," that yeasts had any effect on the wines' flavor. The yeast Blanck likes to use is a powerful strain that will give a nice, fast, clean—uncomplicated—fermentation.

"What about wood?" he asked me defensively. "What about Krug and their Clos de Mesnil? That Champagne is presented as the ultimate mono cru, and of course," he said with false modesty, "I would never compare ours to the *great* Clos de Mesnil, but Krug's house style is barrel fermentation and to keep the wine in wood for a long time. Wood is the worst thing you can do to *terroir*."

I didn't want to engage in battle with Mr. Blanck, but it was getting difficult to hold my tongue. I agree that the overuse of wood is one of the more awful treatments you can give to wine, but my objection is to new wood with heavy toast. Historically, Krug had been fermented in old wood, decades old, in fact. Old wooden barrels allow the Champagne to develop in a fascinating way, allow the wine to mingle with oxygen and evolve with Golden Delicious apple flavors, perhaps a little apple pie and roasted hazelnut. The wood itself at Krug didn't interfere; the oxygen did.

Oh, the quandary: When to speak up and when to hold my tongue? Where is the balance between journalistic truth seeking and truculent banter? I had to navigate myself through lunch without insulting my host. But it sure seemed that Blanck was being unduly catty, knocking the competition (even if owned by the same parent company, Moët Hennessy Louis Vuitton) with a damning and misleading comment, which—he hoped—I didn't know enough to contradict. I tap-danced my way to a new topic.

"And what about farming organically?" I asked.

"Impossible in Champagne," he said. "Just look at this weather. Disease and mildew can be difficult to control." When I pointed to the success of Larmandier-Bernier, Selosse, Jacquesson, and Leclerc Briant—all making organic, single-vineyard Champagnes—Blanck was not impressed. Moët was too huge and made too much wine to work in that way.

I started to pray that Honey-Sugar would throw off the promise of silence I'd made her take and fire up her charm. Obviously I wasn't doing so well on my own.

"I love the Pinot Meunier the best," Honey-Sugar said, piping up. Then she started to gush about the magnificence of the property, with a wonderful excitement and innocence. Blanck, though softened, did not really want to leave the topic under discussion.

"Once in a while a company wants to show its skills," he said. "While we buy grapes from other vineyards, we also own some special pieces of land. We chose three that we own, and we planted each one with a different grape. These wines are from one parcel of land and one kind of grape; however, we do blend vintages."

Then he really started getting wound up. "People didn't understand why we don't make a vintage mono cru. The reason is that we believe that the Champagne identity is about the blend and the consistency you can get from it. We get great marks on the new bottles. Critics love them. But we are not concerned about selling the bottles. We want to show the world that we are not just big, but we are serious vine growers as well."

So, there's the answer. Moët was indeed threatened by the little wine guys; they wanted the connoisseur's vote at the cash register.

It was hard not to remember the words of an expatriot friend in Paris who works intimately with real luxury. "LVMH is all about the look of *luxe*," he'd said, surrounded by samples and mannequins in his Place Vendôme office, drinking espresso and sucking on a cigarette. "Quality has nothing to do with them."

THE NEXT MORNING, the brilliant sun finally warmed the rain chill from my bones. It almost seemed like the July that it was. Honey-Sugar happily slipped her new pink Kenzo shawl—"I can't believe they gave this to me!"—over her sweater and we headed toward Vertus, a town famous for its Chardonnay. By nine in the morning, we were standing in the vines with Pierre Larmandier, who embodies all that is good about the small producer who also makes a mono cru. Pierre has fifty parcels, with twelve hectares (about thirty acres) in Vertus. This is quite a lot. To supplement his income he also sells grapes to some of the big producers. One customer, he said, is Champagne Bollinger. With his wife, Pierre now operates Champagne Larmandier-Bernier on biodynamic principles, and is one of the very few in the region working with indigenous yeast. He makes several Champagne blends and one single-vineyard bottling from a densely chalked plot on his property. "Vertus is on the chalk. There is no topsoil here," he said of his land's *terroir.* "It's chalk all the way through."

The particular vineyard we were standing in was the one from which he makes his mono cru, Terre de Vertus. His neighbor is Clicquot, with its chemically treated, weed-free vineyards. "That's Clicquot?" Honey-Sugar asked as she took in the desolate landscape. Having been her friend for so long, I knew what was going through her mind—her second wedding. It was to be a tiny affair, a dozen of us. Her Parisian husband had insisted on serving Clicquot. That particular husband was always late, and this wedding was no exception. Tired of pacing, the twelve of us finally broke out the Clicquot. His excuse for getting to the *chuppah* two hours late? He was fixing the washing machine.

With that kind of association, it's amazing that Honey-Sugar could have continued to drink the stuff at all. But seeing the Clicquot vineyards cured her for good. Honey-Sugar is the kind of girl who drops several hundred dollars a week on organic food. She stared at the sterile soil under the Clicquot vines with a new understanding.

To get rid of weeds, most people—especially in Champagne— just throw down chemicals instead of plowing the soil. Pierre started to plow in 1992. Influenced by the first Champagne maker to work organically, Anselme Selosse, he saw the wisdom in making wine from healthy dirt. Pierre makes a wine maven's Champagne. Though he's got an international reputation, he gets no respect in his hometown. His uncle, Guy (who was also a maker of "grower" Champagne), lived nearby. At the time of my visit, the two barely spoke. Uncle, who has since passed away, not only condemned his nephew's single-vineyard Champagne, finding it heretical to Champagne's blending ethics, but also disapproved of his wacky winemaking methods. Organic in Champagne? *Mon dieu!*

We retreated to Pierre's tasting room, a modest addition attached to the home where he, his wife, and their children lived. We sat down to a round table in a disheveled room stacked with books and magazines. He opened up a small refrigerator, the kind you'd see in a college dorm, and pulled out a few Champagnes sold in the States from about thirty-five to sixty dollars. "The appellation of Champagne has an obsession with consistency," he told us. "I do not. I want to show the vintage. I want the yearly differences. These are good things. Also, I am not obsessed with acidity and so don't pick underripe. I am not obsessed with control."

Whereas Moët created its mono cru to prove something to the world, the mono cru Né d'une Terre de Vertus was created for the most straightforward of reasons: Pierre realized that the vineyard produced a wine that tasted better on its own than it did as part of a traditional Champagne blend. Whereas the Moët wines had a hollow quality, Terre de Vertus was bubbly and very wine-like, with fresh-bread and salty, sea-air aromas, expressing nutty, deeply rich, layered flavors and minerality.

I watched Honey-Sugar's expression light up. She still hadn't begun to spit, and clearly she didn't want to spit these Champagnes. The 2000 Terre de Vertus has no dosage, the extra sugar typically added before the Champagne is bottled. It is yeasty and real with an extremely fresh, nutty appeal and a squeaky-clean finish.

"This wine took two months to complete fermentation," Pierre told us.

Most fermentations in Champagne, as with Moët's, take under a week. Georges Blanck had said, "I like a fast and clean fermentation." And you probably set your watch by it.

As we walked out to the car, Honey-Sugar was excited, saying, "You can really taste grape in those Champagnes." And then she added, "I will never buy another big-name brand of Champagne again. I hope there are more here like Pierre's."

I told her my shortlist: Selosse. Françoise Bedel. Raymond Brigandat. José Dhondt. Fleury. Pierre Moncuit. Camille Saves. Davide LeClapart. Jacquesson. Jacques Lassaigne. Leclerc Briant. There are plenty of alternatives to the Yellow Labels and Moëts of this world. And, in a pinch, I am also quite fond of Bollinger and can drink Pol Roger, too.

By daybreak, I knew that the chill I'd caught in the Moët vineyards had blossomed in my body as a killer cold. By breakfast, it was clear that Honey-Sugar was getting all of the symptoms I had. I really hoped winemaker Pascal Leclerc Briant would forget all about our appointment.

The phone rang about eleven. It was Pascal. He was expecting me in half an hour. I scrounged in my little packet of travel pills for something useful. Lodged in with the anti–jet lag sleep aids were aspirin and two shiny-red Sudafed pills. *Eureka!* I packed a box of tissues, drank copious amounts of tea, and drove the thirty minutes from Reims to Epernay. Honey-Sugar couldn't move. I had no choice.

It was Sunday. Epernay was gray and still. In direct contrast was the jovial, hyper, bearded, unkempt, silver-haired and blue-eyed Pascal in his leprechaun-green jacket (which, he said, was the color of his winery). Many in Champagne make fun of Pascal. He is a good marketer, they say, and that's why he changed to biodynamics. After all, even the Champagne promotional board considers biodynamics irrelevant, impossible, and a desperate attempt to capture publicity. Pascal is not against promotion, but he is an authentic eccentric and authentically passionate. Yes, his mono cru trio started out as a way to service a market. A group of sommeliers in Paris were searching for a mono cru and thought Pascal's vineyards had the right stuff. So he bottled a trio of multivintage mono cru and, long before Moët got the idea, Pascal had his own *Trilogie,* which he aptly called Les Authentiques.

The wines are not mono-vintage, and they are not mono-grape. The only thing "mono" about them is the one plot of land they come from in the early-maturing village of Cumières. The vineyards Les Chèvres Pierreuse and Les Crayères are planted with a classic mix of the three Champagne grapes. Le Clos de Champions—my favorite of Pascal's Champagnes—is a fifty-fifty mix of Pinot Noir and Chardonnay that has an oxidized, rich style and the toasted-nut aromas that the English love.

Pascal comes to the organic concept quite honestly. His father experimented with organic viticulture back in 1964. Unfortunately, in the first year he lost sixty percent of his production to mildew. Proving the axiom that there are no atheists in a foxhole, he ran back to chemical treatments and to using as much sulfur as needed to stop the mildew. Pascal heard about biodynamics in 1989, and became utterly convinced that grapes grown using its principles made wines that were much more expressive. He understood that the concept of biodynamics was based on maintaining health and balance in the soil, and started to learn. Despite his father's failure with organics, Pascal was ready to take the plunge. He converted his vineyards in 2000, finding that, because of the biodynamic treatments, his vineyards were much healthier, and more easily withstood the Champagne mildew problem.

"Moët," I said, "told me that organic is too expensive and, anyway, not possible in the area."

He made an interesting snort, then laid his theory of why Moët shunned organics. "You pay seven hundred euros per hectare to farm with chemicals. To farm biodynamically, it's one hundred euros more per hectare per year. And then on top of that, labor is five to ten percent more expensive. How many millions of bottles does Moët make?" Pascal's thinking was correct. When you add up the figures, the amount saved by using chemicals is substantial. To convert, Moët would have to make a serious financial commitment to real quality as opposed to the illusion of quality.

Pascal's brain was an unusual place. Spend any time with him at all and you're sure to find out that he holds the record for building the world's largest workable Champagne fountain. (He used 14,404 Champagne flutes.) His is one of the few small Champagne houses equipped to receive visitors. If you inquire ahead, for a tiny fee you can rappel down into his chalk caves, shoot skeet in the vineyards, or learn to "saber" a Champagne bottle. When we came back from his vineyards, he asked me if I wanted to knock the neck off a bottle. Did I! We went up to the second floor, over the winery, and onto the balcony overlooking the backside of Epernay. He handed me the saber, smaller than the one I remembered from a Bastille Day celebration hosted in Soho by Clicquot, which had been double the size of a chef's knife. I practiced sliding it up and down on the bottle, focusing on the weak part, just under the lip of the bottle top. Pascal coached me. "Just take the saber and slice it . . . past the lip. You don't need a lot of strength." I was worried about making a mess, but I shouted like a little kid when I sliced off a bottle top in one swift swoop and the bubbles burbled onto the cement two stories below.

Between his infectious laugh and the shock of the gushing bottle, I forgot about my cold and the emotional funk that had prompted this great summer adventure. Stupid as it may sound, the passion of these growers and the power of their commitment started to make me believe in my future as well.

But my intended short visit had turned into hours—and at last my body was failing as the Sudafed wore off. My fizzy fantasies bled into a dreamlike of craving for more drugs. I longed to go back to the little inn, my comfortable nest at Les Templiers, for sleep.

In the morning, both Honey-Sugar and I were still plagued by stuffed noses and slight fevers. I pulled her out of bed. "You cannot miss this one," I told her. "I don't care how sick you are. You just can't come here and miss Krug. You'll never forgive me." I shared my new drug with her—nose spray made with geranium (the French are big on natural remedies). We trudged off to meet Krug's first winemaker who wasn't a Krug, Nicolas Audebert, at the walled-in vineyard in the center of the village of Mesnil.

I love—or rather *loved*—Krug's regular blend. With its lime-like, thirst-quenching acidity, I never failed to recognize it even when tasting it blind. I admit to favoring it over the Champagne made separately from the Clos de Mesnil vineyard—as Blanck sniffingly conceded, the most famous of the mono crus.

All of the Clos de Mesnil in the world was made from a tiny plot of 4.6 acres planted with Chardonnay, originally in 1698. A wall was built around it for protection. Clos de Mesnil was a legendary Champagne with a legendary price (about 540 dollars per bottle, the world's most expensive). But when I saw the vineyard, I was crushed. I had expected to see it given a little more respect. Here, too, the soil was not plowed, and while it was a bit livelier than Moët's, it wasn't by much. And there were ubiquitous flecks of blue plastic. Honey-Sugar, like a chicken looking for a worm, kept bending down to pick them up.

Clos de Mesnil is sacred ground in Champagne. What would it take to make an example of this teensy bit of property and make a biodynamic vineyard, or at least plow the earth and give it its life back?

Audebert said that this was impossible.

"Why?" I asked.

"Because it is Clos de Mesnil, owned by LVMH—they don't have to," he said with an ironic smile.

"You could at least hire someone to pick up the blue plastic," Honey-Sugar told him. "I know someone over in Boston. She's real cheap and she's really good, if you want her number." She looked at me to see if she was overstepping her bounds. I smiled. She was perfect.

We walked into the barrel room, where Audebert showed off some brand-new oak fermentation tanks, and we tasted two wines out of bottle. First up was the workhorse, my beloved multivintage Krug. The Champagne came in a new package, nice and sleek. I was told there was nothing new inside, but there was. It tasted markedly different. Gone was its tangy lime. Gone was its richness. Gone was its identity. I had heard something was up, and now I knew it to be true.

I did not like this wine. It was no longer my baby. I supposed, in one sense, it was all right. At 130 dollars a pop I couldn't afford Krug. Now it certainly wasn't worth it.

Then came the Clos de Mesnil 1990. It had a strong coconut aspect, a minerality with smoky, toasty edges, and an undertone of mushroom. The note I was most attracted to was ginger. I blurted out, "If the wine is this good, can you imagine what it would be like if the soil were allowed to live?"

Audebert politely asked what I meant.

"Let me put it this way," I said. "Do you have even one earthworm in that soil? Clos is a tiny vineyard. What would it cost to farm organically here and make Krug from soil that has life and vitality?"

Audebert repeated what seemed to be the corporate mantra: Farming organically in Champagne was impossible.

"That's exactly what Georges Blanck said," I told him.

He was amused to hear that I had talked with Blanck, saying, "I worked with him at Moët. Do you know he never tastes when he makes Champagne? It's all done by the numbers."

I remembered Blanck's immaculate hands, and the news did not surprise me.

As we talked about some of his peers and elders who had bet their vineyards on organic farming techniques, Audebert became increasingly excited. I had a fantasy that perhaps young Audebert was jonesing to join these renegades and become a winemaker on the cutting edge of the Champagne New Wave himself. It was a lovely thought, but I realized that defecting from the cushy corporate security of LVMH would be near impossible.

Back in the car, Honey-Sugar's blue eyes almost welled up with tears. "That was so depressing!" she wailed. "I was so looking forward to Krug. Did it really used to be better?"

"It was. Really. It was."

"It's such a shame about that Nicolas," she went on. "Because he is really a handsome man, even with that pompadour he wears. He should make better wine." She paused. "You don't think it's our colds, now, do you?"

"No," I said.

"Pierre's Champagne was better," she concluded. "I'm going back to Boston and getting me some of that. Yum."

SOME TIME AFTER my voyage with Honey-Sugar, I returned to Champagne on my own, where I finally caught up with Richard Juhlin, a Swedish writer specializing in Champagne who had preceded me at the wineries during my earlier visit. "When Moët released their mono-cru wines," he explained, "it meant that the big houses couldn't complain about mono crus anymore; it was a trend they couldn't ignore." He continued. "But tasting through the three of them, I realized that they tasted more like the Moët style than any sort of *terroir.*"

I believe that no matter how much they protest, the Grandes Marqués and their LVMH owners are taking notice, even if they assume that their huge size makes them immune to the growing trend among Champagne lovers to reject the big brand and drink the underdog. Forget the mono-cru stuff: One day, I am sure, the big houses will come out with their own "grower" champagne.

LVMH can afford to have Champagne made by people who never taste the wine. They can afford to change the taste of Krug, and they can afford to abuse their soil. After all, look at the big business their Louis Vuitton brand does with their vinyl-impregnated leather goods—the illusion of *luxe*.

Mireille Guiliano, the woman who now is more famous for her book *French Women Don't Get Fat,* than for her real contribution to popular culture, creating the powerhouse Champagne brand Veuve Clicquot, managed to arrange a lunch for me with the head of Moët Hennessy, Mark Cornell. I wanted to find out something about how the company viewed the "little people" of Champagne. And I wanted to ask him about something else—the big flavor change in Krug.

Cornell is an unlikely ruler of the wine division of Moët Hennessy, but this sort of incongruity has become commonplace at LVMH. For instance, Cécile Bonnefond was hired away from Sara Lee to run Clicquot. When LVMH hired Cornell he, too, lacked any previous connection to wine.

An imposing man, Cornell had an impeccable British accent, which he put to good use—he was a fantastic raconteur. We talked wine. He confessed that he had never believed in wine until he had his moment of wine truth. "I was a professional soldier for eight years, and I was kind of an angry young man. I was in a bar and eavesdropping on this man trying to impress his date by telling her of his experience with the wine in his glass. He smelled, inhaled, commented, 'Chablis is so flinty, can you smell it?' I just couldn't stand it. The man was so pretentious. I turned around and told him he was full of crap. There was no way he could tell the difference. And when was the last time he sucked on flint? Then I told him that I was a soldier and had smelled flint for eight years. But a few years later, I was out with a very attractive woman. I had a glass of Chablis in my hand. I put my nose in it, and it smelled like flint! . . . After that, I was a believer."

He told me how excited he was to be taking Krug into the twenty-first century. LVMH had initially hired him to revamp the cognac house Hine. "But for LVMH to take over Hine meant to ruin it," he said. "It is a small house. A fine house. I couldn't ruin the brand. So I updated it and found a good buyer. We could have made more money by selling it to a Russian firm, but we went with less money and a better buyer."

I said, "To take a phrase from the sixties, 'If you love it let it go?'" He was polite to laugh, because it really wasn't funny. From his story I gleaned that he thought he couldn't bring himself to ruin Hine—but Krug? Perhaps that he could ruin.

We ordered our mediocre lunch. I had some peppered tuna salad, he had lobster bisque, and we shared a half bottle of Krug. Even though this Krug had a newer label, it still tasted just as I remembered. He and I both decided it was delicious and mused that the restaurant might have had it lying around for a few years, and it probably had some bottle age on it.

I couldn't have asked for a better segue. I told him my observation that Krug didn't seem like Krug anymore. He told me that a number of people had similarly complained to him about a change, so many that he took the allegations seriously. He marched into headquarters in Reims and demanded to know what nefarious changes were afoot. Remi, one of the two Krug brothers (who had sold their shares to LVMH and were now just on salary), told him that, of course there's been a change. In a fake French accent, Cornell mimicked Remi and his scornful explanation. "There's new packaging, so everyone assumes what is inside the bottle is different!"

"But the change in taste is true," I said. "At least to my palate it is true. This bottle was an exception, but every other time I've had Krug in the past two years I've been terribly disappointed. It was always the only Champagne I could guess in a blind tasting. The limelike acidity was such a tell, and now that and its complexity are gone."

He said that was impossible. The only difference was the label.

I talked about it with Parker, and even he caught the difference, though he couldn't quite nail it down. Jancis Robinson, the perspicacious British wine critic, who (to my thinking) has a far superior palate, had similar Krug difficulties. In January 2006, she reported her findings in a blind tasting on her Web site.

I can only assume that this potentially great wine is being released at a much earlier stage than previously. For the moment,

I would counsel people to avoid this cuvée (distinguishable by its new cream- rather than maroon-dominated label), or at least cellar it for at least a couple of years. Tasting it blind I suspected it was a youthful Bollinger. Perhaps the wine was discombobulated by being decanted, but I can't believe that it could possibly have tasted gorgeous straight from the bottle. A great disappointment. Go for those older bottles!

Krug, RIP. I was spoiled enough to know it wasn't the same. At that lunch Cornell told me that Nicolas Audebert had been moved to Argentina, where he would make nonsparkling wines. Georges Blanck was gone, too, moved, he couldn't tell me where.

I was very curious where M. Blanck went, so I did some inquiring and found out the most fascinating thing. The American-brand director, Erica Kwei, told me that Blanck, had become *"directeur du développement durable,"* responsible for leading the company's efforts in sustainable practices.

Was this some sort of joke? Was this an LVMH twist of irony? Were they pulling my leg? Wasn't it Blanck who'd told me that farming organically in Champagne was impossible? Even though sustainable agriculture is based on chemical farming, I felt that putting Blanck in charge of sustainable practices is like giving Paris Hilton a contract to write a book on modesty. No one could tell me what changes Blanck was actually making.

Pierre Larmandier had spoken with so much passion about the expression of the soil: Whether making a blend or a mono cru, he made a wine first, one with a unique expression of the *terroir* from which it sprang, whereas companies like Moët make a *brand* first. It's a big difference. Without *terroir,* a wine holds no interest for Pierre. He is part of the real Champagne revolution—something that, even in the mouths of babes like my friend Honey-Sugar, can't be ignored.

– 6 –

Desperately Seeking
Scanavino

I was determined to visit the grave, deathbed, children, wife, house, anything that could give me some insight into the man who made the first wine to make me realize I was in the presence of an indefinable force. I refer, of course, to that first Barolo, pinched from my father's mistress's ex-husband, that 1968 Giovanni Scanavino. Because I know that my friend Elena, a fierce woman (with a world-class head of horsetail hair) who runs an organic cooperative outside Alba, is as stubborn as a dog with a bone when she has a job to do, she was the first one I assigned to the task. She wrote me in response.

Dear Alice,

The Scanavino company went out of business in the 1980s (they made more Barolo than all of the Barolo that is produced today in the Barolo appellation: This helps you to understand what the quality of their wine was like!!!). The company

139

changed ownership twice. Mr. Giovanni Scanavino lives in Priocca, doesn't work anymore, and is very ill. His sons work in the furnishing business. One is a lawyer.

Affectionately, Elena

I was so excited. I called the Skinny Food Writer to share the news. "He's alive! Elena found him!"

"Goodie," Skinny said.

"And Elena said he made terrible wine!" I shouted. "Isn't that fabulous?"

The Skinny Food Writer was confused. "Why is that so great?"

"Don't you get it?" I tried to explain. "The first Barolo to steal my soul was made by a bad winemaker. That is just so terrific." I couldn't stop laughing. This was the biggest joke on wine snobbery ever.

I did a little digging into the writings of Sheldon (Shelly) Wasserman, who is still cited as one of the great chroniclers of Italian wine. He died in 1990 at the young age of fifty-one. His book *Italy's Noble Red Wines* was released the year of his death. In it, he wrote about the Scanavino wines, "Cannot recommend except to avoid." The irony that I, the wine writer who swears by her nose and palate, had loved a crappy wine was precious. I now had proof that from my earliest wine-geek moment I would rather drink a pretechnology wine—even if it was considered lousy—than one of the high-scoring, modern, spoofulated wines. I decided to stitch the Scanavino mission onto a visit to VinItaly, the big, blowout wine show in the town Shakespeare made famous, Verona. Even better, there were to be a few fringe wine tastings near VinItaly dedicated to natural wines.

This fringe-wine-fair trend had started several years back, outside of the biggest wine trade show of them all, Bordeaux's VinExpo. VinExpo, like most gargantuan trade shows, is held in a sterile pavilion bathed with painful fluorescent light and filled with bad air. Many of the wines exhibited are conventional ones presented by marketers instead of winemakers. Discoveries exist in between the aisles; it just requires awfully hard work to suss them out. The fringes, on the other hand, are much smaller satellite gatherings filled with independent winemakers who share like-minded philosophies and without one trace of the Big Wine cartel—no Diageo, LVMH, or Pernot Ricard.

The hot, muggy year I had visited VinExpo, I found myself so overwhelmed by the traffic and the crowds that I spent all of my time taking refuge at the fringe tastings, especially one particular tasting under tents overlooking the hills of Canon Fronsac. There I discovered fantastic vignerons, ate and drank well, got caught in a miraculous lightning storm, ended up drenched, and loved every minute of it. So after a few years when there was nothing going on in Verona besides the big VinItaly, it was heartening to hear that the fringe trend had breached the country. There were to be three fringe fairs. *Progress!* The shows were going to be pan-European, and while I knew the wines would be predominantly French, I was certain I'd find rebel Italian winemakers who had escaped my watchful eyes, Italians who worked without the tools of spoofulation.

"I'm coming on this trip," Skinny said. "I don't care whether or not I get an assignment, there's no way I'm missing a chance to meet Giovanni and go to Verona."

To convince Giovanni Scanavino to grant me an audience, I would need the help of my Italian-speaking friends. I spared Francesco because he'd already helped me so much in the Rhône. I spared Elena because she had already done some work on the case. I decided to try Lars, who works for Long Island–based Villa Banfi importers and the owners of Castello Banfi in Montalcino, Tuscany.

Lars reported back. "Nope. Signore Scanavino won't see you." He said that Giovanni's wife confirmed that her husband was sick and wouldn't see anyone. Lars also snooped among his other Piedmontese contacts, and said that no one was giving him any details but—because they were being cagey—he sensed a "Scandalavino"!

Then I asked Dr. J., my friend in a faux-French band who has a Ph.D. in Italian and also works in the wine business. The son of a psychiatrist, Dr. J. is capable of finessing virtually any situation with seamless ease. Consider the time I asked him to come along to dinner with an Umbrian wine producer, Marco Caprai. The Caprais make wine from the Sagrantino grape, which grows nowhere else in the world except in the town of Montefalco. The highly unusual grape produces an exceedingly tannic wine. Despite the tongue-ripping tannins, though, it is filled with sun-ripe fruit when made well. I find the wine wild and compelling. Here's the catch: Though I love the wines from the Bea, Napolini, Antonelli, and Antano wineries in Montefalco, I find that Caprai's are undrinkable—*molto spufulato.*

The Caprais are the rich family in town. I once asked why they make their wine with so much wood, and Marco said, "If you are poor you use old barrel, if you are rich you use *barrique.* We are rich."

Nevertheless, the family has done much to promote the Sagrantino grape and the area. At the dinner, Dr. J. said to our host, "You're the Biondi-Santi of Montefalco!" referring to the producer who made Brunello famous. This was like telling Marco he was to Montefalco what Jesus Christ was to Catholicism. The compliment had the desired effect. The winemaker spread his hands over his chest and sprouted a beatific grin, as if to say, "Yes! Dr. J., my brother. You understand!"

Afterward, I asked Dr. J. why he'd toyed with Marco that way. After all, we really were not fans of his wines. And Dr. J. said, "Because I could."

So it shouldn't have surprised me that right before I was to leave for Italy, I got this note from Dr. J.

I just spoke to Scanavino's wife . . . She said that he did make that wine. I told her that you'd like to meet, the whole story, the book, etc. She said that her husband is sick and they would have to think about it. She said to call when you're in Italy. Seems like a meeting is possible, although it'll depend on his health . . . He was in bed with a fever, his wife told me . . . She was nice and open to the idea.

With hope in the air, I took to chanting while doing my pliés in ballet class: *"Come on, Giovanni, baby cakes. Agree to see me!"*

Excited, Skinny and I flew out of Newark. With the Jersey shore beneath us, I slid out our airplane wine. The "juice" in my seltzer bottle was Clos Roche Blanche Côt, 2004, my good luck charm. The Skinny Food Writer brought a delicious, lemony broccoli salad she was testing for a cookbook. We munched olives and goat cheese.

"Hey," I said, "did I tell you Big Joe is going to VinItaly and the fringes? I have his schedule. Maybe we'll hook up with him."

We then popped our Ambiens (this time mine was in my wallet, where it belonged) and woke up at landing.

A handkerchief of pea-soupy fog drapes over Milan most mornings, making driving difficult, but not this time. Zipping along at 140 kilometers an hour in the clear, buttercup light, Skinny and I anticipated an easy two-hour ride from Milan. But we missed the turnoff, and all of a sudden we were lost in Gravelona. We were saved by two fantastically handsome consiglieries, who set us straight. Soon we were on the two-lane road from Asti to Alba, where spring had just burst the tree blossoms into popcornlike fluffs. The air was freshly pollened. Nature was in the process of making nature.

Now, maybe it's because the Langhe hills of Piedmont are home to the best white truffles in the world and that close-to-my-heart wine grape, Nebbiolo. Maybe I love the staunch loyalty and passion of the locals. But there is something in the area and in the people of northern Italy that suits me. I first flew there the night of the 2000 presidential election. In the air, the pilot informed us that Gore had won. By the time I drove myself to Alba, Bush had claimed victory. Then we were in the political Ping Pong that divided the nation for weeks. It didn't take long for me to discover that Piedmont had its own split going on: It was the modernist against the traditionalist, and the modernists had won.

It's not much of a stretch to observe that the grape name Nebbiolo comes from the Italian word for the region's morning fog—*nebbia*. Though Nebbiolo grows in other areas of northern Italy and is used in Barbaresco, Ghemme, and Gattinara, its most regal expression is birthed in Barolo from a collection of eleven hilly communes surrounding the town of Alba, in the province of Cuneo. The best of the best come from the vineyards of Barolo, Serralunga d'Alba, La Morra, and Castiglione Falletto.

Nebbiolo is a late-ripening, thin-skinned, tannic grape that just loves those Langhe hills, rich in gypsum, limestone, and marl, which undoubtedly add to the grape's perfume. In youth, Barolos can be as silent as one of those nonverbal guys that have driven me crazy in the past. But give them a little time, a little encouragement, and the wine will become a veritable chatterbox of a philosopher.

While now bracingly dry, it wasn't always that way. Around 1850, the forward-thinking Marquise Giulietta Falletti of Barolo called in a French consultant, Louis Oudart, to figure out why the wines wouldn't finish dry. Oudart determined that the problem was basic: The grapes needed to be healthier. The marquise needed to clean up the cellars and wait a little longer for nature to take its course. Nothing but sound winemaking wisdom.

What might be considered classic Barolo came into being along with my fellow baby boomers in the 1950s. *Traditional* back then meant wine made with a longish (fifteen to forty days) fermentation. Then the wines were aged further, from two to eight years, in large barrels called *botti,* made of Slavonian oak or chestnut (before the 1950s, the wines aged mostly in glass demijohns, like the ones I saw at UC Davis). Every once in a while, aging took longer. For example, the 1970 Giacomo Conterno wasn't bottled until 1984!

There are a few theories for how the French *barrique* came to be used in Piedmont, but fingers point to California as the chief source of the change. In the 1970s, a group of Italian producers visited California and saw the small, French *barriques* and experienced the flavor the barrels could give to a wine. The first sightings of *barriques* in Piedmont were in 1978. There was plenty of initial resistance, but when the Barolo producers saw how the heretofore unmarketable Barbera sold in America after the first few producers switched to *barriques,* they were convinced.

Marco de Grazia, an American living in Florence, is attributed with aiding in the area's modernization. He encouraged many growers who supplied the large producers like Scanavino to make their own wines, and make them according to his guidance. Most of that stable of winemakers—Scavino, Sandrone, Seghesio— became Parker superstars. They made their wines with *barriques,* specialty yeasts, and fermenters that beat up the grapes to make the wine fruitier. By 1990, those new techniques and French barrels had become pandemic. Barbera is a low-tannin grape, and the extra wood did indeed give the wines more structure. Nebbiolo, on the other hand, has high tannin and its wine can have bones. To me, the new wood on Barolo gives the wine hard-edged tannins that feel raspy, as if steel bristles were brushing the back of my throat, ruining the gorgeous wine.

During my first Piedmont visit, I became friendly with the Ceretto family, prominent winemakers, art collectors, and modern Barolo advocates. They were kind enough to help arrange appointments, allowing me to use their office as a home base, and their office assistant, Bruna, helped to make my bookings. I had an appointment with the world-famous Angelo Gaja (a controversial figure and a Parker darling, who had been at the forefront of modern Barolo). On the morning of the appointment, it hit me. I should be making a pilgrimage to the master Barolo maker Bartolo Mascarello. After all, he was my kind of Barolo guy, a legend in town and known for being one of the few holdouts against the nasty *barriques*. Bruna made my cancellations and apologies, but from the look on her face, I knew that she wanted to paddle me.

Mascarello's winery and home are in the village of Barolo itself. Bartolo's only child, Maria Teresa, greeted me. She was not quite as elfin as Maria José in Rioja, but just as spirited. Bartolo sat in his wheelchair with colored pencils before him, drawing wine labels that celebrated his cause: SAY NO TO BARRIQUE. He had the same paper-white skin as his daughter and a similarly proud nose, upon which sat black horn-rimmed glasses. With his daughter translating, Bartolo ranted about Angelo Gaja, he railed against adding grapes like Cabernet to make the color purple, which though illegal, was a common trick. A partisan during World War II, he still had the spirit of a revolutionary.

He conceded that he had tasted modern wines that were "nice," but in Piedmont he wanted to make wines that tasted like his region, not like a wine from anywhere else. I was in love with this old man.

I managed to stay in Bartolo's company for hours. In between the talk and lively debate, his daughter, who at that time had taken over making the wine, took me down to the wine cellar. I had yet to see or smell the funky, spongy black yeasts said to be found hugging wine cellar walls, but here they were, in their beautiful, textural glory—in vivid contrast to modern wineries, with their gleaming, temperature-controlled facilities. Here, temperature control meant an ancient mercury thermometer on the wall and doors that could be opened or closed, depending on whether warmth or chill was desired. Not a small barrel in sight. There were large, old oak and chestnut barrels, and cement vats that looked like relics from Stalinist Russia. This was the very kind of winery, with its "dirty" barrels that both de Grazia and Parker had waged war on. But to me, the musty walls covered in spongy mold, and the wood barrels stained with time created the perfect *mise-en-scène* for making Barolo.

Both de Grazia and Parker forgot to note that *old* and *traditional* do not invariably mean bad wine. Real dirt on the floor does not necessarily mean a winery is unsanitary. Great winemakers like Bartolo have always had similar beliefs and practices: using tender care in the vineyards, keeping yields low, and taking their time in the wine cellar. Cleaning things up and replacing old equipment, they knew, did not translate into better wine, just more predictable wine.

At the end of my visit, Bartolo opened up a bottle of his 1986, which he'd had in his office, waiting for me. The wine was my first Mascarello, and in the wine was sandalwood, suede, tar, and dried roses.

I stayed until the sun set. After all, visiting the master was an historic event. I could have listened to him talk forever. As everything did during that November, conversation turned to American politics—I had already been in Italy for over a week, and there was still no clear presidential winner. Bartolo's vote went to the Democrats. "In an election, Gaja is Bush and I am Gore," he said. As I took my leave, he said to give his regards to Signore Ceretto. "He's a capitalist, but he is a good man." Bartolo thumped his chest and said the only English words he knew: "Last of the Mohicans."

Like Maria José in Rioja he too liked thinking that he was the last. Or, perhaps he just liked taking the spotlight, because he must have known that there was a group of old-timers and anti-*barrique* boys that included Giacomo Conterno, Bruno Giacosa, Giacomo Fenocchio, Teobaldo Cappellano, and Bartolo's own cousin Giuseppe Rinaldi. A small club, but at least it existed.

Now I was back in Piedmont. Skinny was with me. Bartolo was dead. We were playing detective, looking for Scanavino. The

Ceretto family would again be hosting, putting us up in the guest lodging underneath their winery in Castiglione Falletto, smack in the middle (literally) of their Bricco Rocche vineyard. We were meeting the daughter Roberta to get the keys over lunch. By driving us up on sidewalks and in the wrong direction down one-way lanes, I got us to our lunch spot in the middle of town.

Roberta Ceretto's pixie haircut, large green eyes, and white skin exaggerated her little-girl fragility. "Why is it you want to find this Giovanni Scanavino?" she asked.

When I told the boring story of it all, she digested it and then said, "The Scanavino Barolo was famous. He was famous but not important." Did she mean *infamous*? "I'll call Bruna," she added. "She will know everything."

Ever since I had asked the terrifying Bruna to cancel the appointment with Angelo Gaja, she'd had it in for me. But Roberta still got information out of her. My Giovanni was a bad producer; he went into bankruptcy in 1980. Then something jogged Roberta's memory. It seemed that she herself knew the son, a lawyer, and volunteered to call him up. When she got off the phone, she said, "It's very sad. His father is sick and doesn't want to see anyone. I'm sorry."

A nap before dinner was imperative. I crawled into the Ceretto's perfectly crisp linen sheets until the prescribed time for the walk into Castiglione Falletto to forage for dinner. The town itself was no bigger than the cul-de-sac on Long Island where I was brought up. We found our restaurant, Le Torre, framed by two just-in-bloom persimmon trees. Two women alone, we were given the best seats in the house, facing the remarkable hills. It was too dark to see a thing.

In the spirit of division of duty, Skinny looked at the menu while I handled the wine list. Le Torre's was filled with moderately priced good bottles. If I couldn't find an older Barolo I could afford, I was looking for a Nebbiolo, from the 2002 vintage. Why? The weather defines a vintage, and 2002 stank. There was a terribly wet summer. Then the hail came, destroying most of the crop. Prior to 1995, such a disaster would have moved reputable Barolo producers to declassify their wine—meaning that all remaining Nebbiolo grapes were considered not up to the standards for Barolo and would be bottled as Nebbiolo. People like me love bad years—they yield great bargains for the consumer. The trick is to buy the best producer you can in a bad year. I saw a Cavallotto Nebbiolo for eighteen euros. The price was right, and Cavallotto was a local from this very village. I didn't really know him but had heard a rumor that, despite working with importer Marco de Grazia, he was a traditional producer. I asked for the wine. The waiter disappeared and reappeared with a different bottle of wine and a pretty, milkmaidlike woman wearing chef clogs—also his wife—to interpret for him. He talked to her excitedly in Italian, too quickly for me to understand. "Um," the pretty chef said, "this wine is made by Livia Fontana. She is, um, just down the road. I propose to you because she, too, is a traditional wine-maker. Is same price. You like?"

I loved that her husband intuited that my asking for Cavallotto meant I was interested in drinking an older-style wine, not one tricked up for early consumption. How many times have I asked a sommelier in America for a "traditional wine" only to be poured something that has been rotor-fermented, poked, prodded, and *barriqu*ed? But this time instant intimacy via wine speak was achieved. *Only connect!* The Fontana was a lovely little wine, violetty, sanguine, rusty, with a scent of dried rose petals, good sandy tannins, no doubt more Barolo than Nebbiolo. Skinny and I were tired but very happy girls.

At the end of the meal, I asked the chef, who had come out to present each dish as if this were a three-star restaurant, if she knew our friend Alan Tardi, a chef himself, who splits his time between Italy and New York. "Yes!" she said with excitement, almost jumping up and down, fidgeting with her fingers as she tried to find the words she wanted. Alan helped her in the kitchen when he was in town. Between the wine and the food and the connections, Skinny and I had a major love fest, and all for twenty euros apiece.

We were so happy by the time we left Le Torre that we were not too flipped out about heading back into the unfortunate-smelling Ceretto bunker. We woke in the morning to the *nebbia*—the fog swaddled the village like a baby.

I had promised Skinny a trip to meet my friend Elena, she of Cascina del Cornale, an organic-cooperative store/*agritourismo* restaurant on the road between Alba and Asti. Elena has given growers of organic products an important forum, something previously unknown in northern Italy. She has been called the Alice Waters of Italy.

We met on my 2000 trip, the same one on which I met Bartolo. Again, there was a bit of a language problem. I spoke no Italian. She spoke no English. We decided on French and then, frustrated with that option, ended up on the phone, her English-speaking friend interpreting at the other end. It's amazing how a friendship can be forged when both parties have a shared passion but no shared language.

Whenever I visit her, she has some crazy plan for me; sometimes it's an ambush. Like the time she locked me in a room with one of her winemakers, a nice man who believed in growing beautiful grapes but was abusing his wine with spicy oak, designer yeasts, and enzymes. "I want to make a wine Robert Parker would like," he explained. Then Elena instructed me: *"Tell him. Tell him how to make his wine!"* He called his product organic but, like American winemakers who say they grow organically, he kind of missed the point. Though his grapes were organic, his process was processed, and the resulting wine tasted more like cookie dough than the noble grape Nebbiolo. Yet how could I, not a winemaker, tell this man how to make wine? I decided to try an analogy. "It's like a writer who is trying to find a voice," I told him. "You must find your own voice and not make a wine for someone else's palate." It wasn't my most comfortable moment.

Cascina del Cornale is in a rundown farmhouse on a busy commercial road. Geraniums were hanging, and there was plenty of activity in the store when Skinny and I arrived. Elena wasn't yet there, but her assistant Simona pressed us: "First you must have lunch." She had to insist?

We sat outside in the scrubbed sunlight. The restaurant was packed with families happily passing plates of food and drinking. They were drinking what I would have expected, nothing as grand as Barolo or even Barbaresco, but the local choices for everyday wine, Dolcetto, Freisa, Barbera, and Pelaverga.

A plate of variously shaped salami slices appeared, and Skinny was happy. We fawned like proud mothers over a plate of gorgeous, brown, crisp artichoke-and-nettle latkes on a bed of tender, bitter arugula and the cooperative's raw-milk cheeses. Then Elena showed up, speaking vastly improved English. "Now, tell me again why you want see Scanavino."

I went through the spiel. "Tell him all I want is to have him talk to me about Barolo in the seventies. What the wine back then was like, the trends. How the wine was made. Please also tell him that his 1968 changed my life. How can he refuse that one?"

Elena didn't think he could resist, either. "I'll call his wife again," she promised. Of course, in the meantime she put me to work. "Taste these eight wines and tell me what you think," she commanded. Then she revealed the next task on our program. The young pup who made the wines showed up to take us to the Barbaresco hills for a visit to his winery. I groaned inwardly: *She wants me to convert another one.*

In about ten minutes we were pulling onto one of the back roads. "You see that big compound down there?" he asked, pointing. The winery compound looked like the huge Gallo of Sonoma complex. "That's Gaja's. Do you know what Gaja means? *Happy.* If I made all that money, I'd be happy, too."

Our young host had recently taken over his grandfather's winery, which was nothing more than a glorified garage. This young man from rural Piedmont told me that he'd grown up with California and Australia wines and didn't know anything about the older style of local wine. He told us that, in wine school, they taught him how to enzyme, yeast, and inoculate a wine with bacteria for malolactic fermentation. Malolactic is something that develops naturally and can usually be sparked by nothing more than warming up the cellar.

He went on. Because he, like everyone who goes through winemaking school, was terrified of "bad yeast," he was yeasting. And he previously used enzymes as well, but now he didn't want to spend the money. He had made three vintages. His wines were brash and enthusiastic, and it was easy to feel the winemaker as opposed to the weather and the land. I saw a bunch of old barrels and cement tanks and asked him about them. "I still have my grandfather's equipment," he answered. "If you are Piedmontese, you never throw anything out."

Maybe I could influence him, I thought, especially since he kept holding on to the old, perhaps even to old ideas. People can change their points of view. When my friend Catherine Roussel took over her father's Loire winery at twenty-two years of age she, too, yeasted and machine harvested, but she and her wine-making partner realized how much better their wines could be, and they changed. Now their wines are filled with spark and verve.

Our program was not over. We were still captive. The young man had been instructed to take us to a gypsum museum. "Then

Elena will pick you up and take you to Priocca," he promised. "She's kidding, right?" asked Skinny, who was starting to yawn.

If the cost of meeting Scanavino was enduring a plaster museum, I figured, *I can deal.* Anyway, I had been hearing about Elena's obsession with the ancient gypsum moldings found throughout the region for several years. As it turned out, the museum visit provided a firm lesson on the area's *terroir.* The museum was filled with carvings made from the region's gravelly, crumbly, grayish limestone. They were extremely beautiful, and I appreciated how porous they were, how elegantly they accepted color washes. I felt that I finally understood what kind of effect this soil had on Barolo and the people who lived there. Those moldings were drawn from the soil, just as the grapes that grow in the area feed on that gypsum. There is something in that gray limestone matter that makes the flavor of Nebbiolo grown here unlike that grown any other place in the world.

True to her word, Elena soon showed up to claim us. We gave the museum caretaker a tip and got into the car, where she told me the grave news. "Scanavino won't meet with you. I told him it would be good for him. But he is too disgraced."

Disappointed? Oh, yes. I was tempted to give in to the impulse to break down in tears, camp out on his doorstep, bring him flowers and chocolate, and beg. But when mentioning this to Elena, I quickly saw that such a tack would be a total waste of time. A consultation with my schedule told me that we were due at winemaker Teobaldo Cappellano's in Serralunga d'Alba. What would I rather do? Be pathetic on someone's doorstep or meet a fabulous winemaker who maybe could give me further insight?

On the way to Cappellano's, I was self-absorbed. Until that moment I had almost convinced myself that this adventure would all work out—we'd meet Scanavino and solve the mystery of the scandal. Now it all seemed like an expensive fiasco. Sweetly, Skinny was trying to make me feel better. "It's okay not to see him, it's fine," she said. "It's even better if you don't see him. It's the journey that matters."

How Zen.

But now I very much wanted to know the secret: What *was* the damned Scandalavino? I wanted to know which part of Giovanni was able to make that 1968. Was I behaving like a foolish woman who falls in love with a man because he has potential? Was it like my relationship with the Owl Man? A difficult one, for sure, but there were such moments of joy and deep understanding and connection; why couldn't the Owl Man and I build on those blocks of extreme good? How did that potential get into my 1968, and how did it get lost? Ping Pong. In love and wine, I went back and forth.

I drove up to the town of Serralunga, looking for Baldo's house. In fact, I drove up and down and up and down and up and down, and then I gave up and pulled onto the shoulder of the road in front of someone's house. I got out of the car and gaped at the scene across the road, the chemically burned vineyards of Piedmont's largest producer, Fontanafredda. Hadn't anyone told them that chemicalizing the life out of the soil was no longer fashionable? Their soil could have been in Champagne, it was so bereft. Then I saw a gentleman in a T-shirt and suspenders in front of a neighbor's house. I called out to him, "*Scusi, dov'é* Baldo Cappellano?" He pointed me to the Art Nouveau, wrought-iron gate I was parked in front of. It's like that all the time in Italy. I'm lost, only to find I'm not. But no one was home. He must have given up on us and went into the vineyards. We waited and waited. Skinny worked and I paced, until his car pulled in. A tall man who looked like Jimmy Carter ushered us into the tiny farmhouse that housed his very cramped winery. I liked Baldo. He seemed to be one of those gentle giants, long and weedy, dressed in cords, flannel shirt, and ratty sweater. *Here is another Piedmontese character,* I thought, *like Bartolo and Elena.*

Once inside, he mentioned his few nods to modernity, like stainless-steel tanks. I looked around. "But you don't have any," I said.

"I thought they were ugly, so I covered them in wood," he answered. He told us some charming local history, such as that land used to be measured in something called *giornata*—the time it took for a cow to eat the grass. Eventually the talk turned from his wines to the Italian election, to Berlusconi's plastic surgery, and finally to sex and love.

"There are women you love and women you want to be the mother of your children," he stated. "It is the same with wine. Look, up the road to Serralunga there is Swiss man who has cows and sells milk. I love that milk, straight from the cow. But I can't always get there. Sometimes I have to go to the supermarket. There has to be room for both kinds of milk and both kinds of wine. Here is the crime: Industry pretends to be artisan, and trusting people believe them. This is the crime, yes. Antinori makes thirty million bottles, and he wants to be seen as an artisan. Gaja is a small producer? Of course, he only makes *two million* bottles. It's stupid. Of course, many of these wines are made popular by Mr. Parker." Baldo finished up. "It's not that we should kill Mr. Parker, but sometimes we must break his pencil."

We said our good-byes, promising to visit him at ViniVeri. Helping to organize the alternative wine tasting was one of the ways Baldo was helping to break Mr. Parker's pencil.

There was one more important visit to make before we headed south to Verona and the madhouse of VinItaly.

Bartolo had been dead for a couple of years, and I wanted to see what had changed now that Maria Teresa didn't have her father around to disapprove of any modernization.

Since I last saw her, six years earlier, Maria Teresa had grown into a female version of her father, her blond hair now gray, a hipper version of her father's clunky glasses sitting on her proud Bartolo nose. She squinted at me, trying to remember who I was. *"Ah, sisi."* Whether or not she remembered, she was gracious. She now sat in her father's place behind the desk. Everywhere were his hand-drawn labels. Much was exactly as he left it. For example, she still had not given in to the lure of computers. She used a fax machine. She did, however, have a bathroom, which I asked to use. I walked through the kitchen, where her mother,

Bartolo's widow, was making a heavenly smelling lunch—of what, I do not know, but the smell of it must have reached down into Bartolo's grave. The wall in the bathroom was covered in anti-Bush and anti-Berlusconi cartoons. Yes, this was indeed the house Bartolo built. When I returned to the office, Maria Teresa started to go at it, punctuating her words with her long, expressive fingers. First, she attacked the loss of biodiversity in the area. Then she got on to global warming, and how the combination of heat and the crazy practice of leaving grapes on the vine so long were driving wine alcohols dangerously high. Then she circled back home to the modernists and the *barriques*. She was on a roll.

"And now, now we have biodynamics—I laugh at them," she said with scorn. "The producers who first sprayed chemicals are now *pretending* to spray herbs. Don't get me wrong. I don't mean to be cynical about biodynamics. I'm not saying yes, I'm not saying no. But now it is a fashion for producers to gaze at the moon once and say, 'Look at me, I am biodynamic.' To be fully biodynamic is a religion, yet there are people using the *fashion* of biodynamics for marketing."

She went on. "I have to sell wine. I have a business to run. I can't farm with a horse. I can't bury horns filled with manure in the ground. It is not either biodynamic or use chemicals. It is not one thing or another. Now we go from super-high-tech wines to wines that are too funky to be real? Do you know, people come up to me and ask me why I use sulfur?"

She raised issues that I, too, tussle with. I, too, am fearful biodynamics and natural wines will become the next marketing darling. It has already started. The visuals of biodynamics, with the moon and with animals running around in the vines, are a marketer's dream. All advertising agencies would have to do is snap a picture with some horns in the background and the new drinker, curious about biodynamics, would make the leap to natural.

"Journalists don't help," Maria Teresa continued accusingly, catching me off guard. "They don't promote tradition and *terroir*."

Skinny tried to come up to my rescue, to speak on my behalf, but I *shush*ed her. I tried not to take it personally—I wanted to take the topic myself.

"Who has been the most detrimental to the state of Barolo?" I asked. "The *Wine Spectator*? Parker? Marco de Grazia or French wine consultants?"

She laughed. She found the questions so amusing. "All of them go in the same direction of modern Barolo. But all of them needed to learn from Luigi Veronelli," she said, referring to the late, prominent Italian wine critic. "He was the only one who had the knowledge to review wines. I do not like this American way, the Parker way of judging wine. It takes the wine from the place. Veronelli connected the culture to wine. That is the way it needs to be done. Do you know, the *Wine Spectator*'s James Suckling said my wine smelled like a room with two dogs in it!"

I actually had had my own tasting of that 2001 Barolo, to which the *Wine Spectator* gave an 84. My friend Dr. J. slipped it into a blind lineup with three other wines. When the wines were unveiled, the Bartolo Mascarello turned out to be the most pure and certainly the one most loved. It was young. No hint of any dogs in a room, as the *WS* wrote. What I did find was a little pickle under the flowery, cherry aroma. Missing for me as far as classic notes go was some licorice. I was confused by the tannins. There were wood tannins mixed in with the mostly rustic Barolo tannins I love so well. I'm not used to that in the Mascarello wine. I wondered if this was the first year she'd used replacement barrels. The trouble is that all wood must be new at one point. There is no getting around it. But in time, and Mascarello is around for the long haul, the wine will win over the wood.

"There's something we've been trying to figure out on this trip. What is the soul of Barolo?" I asked.

This topped my last question; Maria Teresa was seriously amused. She laughed hard. But then she lifted her chin. "Barolo is a very old and high soul. It's not just now, people have been always trying to steal and corrupt the soul of Barolo. Before the laws governing the wines, they used to use wines from Puglia. There are still laws in effect about winemaking. Cabernet or Petite Verdot is not allowed in Barolo, yet people do use them. There has always been and always will be manipulation."

Ever since people figured out how to stomp grapes, wine has been manipulated. Champagne and wines made with bubbles are oft-used examples of highly manipulated wines. Some, like California's Clark Smith of the reverse-osmosis, micro-oxygenation machines, argue that without manipulation there would be no wine. That is their argument for the use of technology. But when does manipulation rob the soul of a wine? It's an old story: Syrah from the Rhône was shipped to Bordeaux, and Pugliese grapes were shipped to Piedmont. Every generation has its story of wine adulteration. The battle for a wine's soul isn't a new one at all, and now won't be the last time the battle is waged, either.

Finally, I asked the inevitable. "Do you know someone named Giovanni Scanavino?"

She narrowed her pale eyes. She asked musically, *"Priocca?"*

"Si," I said, flaunting my impeccable Italian.

She said, "I know nothing."

In the car, the Skinny Food Writer exclaimed, "How could she not know?"

"Her father would have known," I lamented. "I wish I had asked him when I had the chance."

"But," Skinny said, "he wouldn't have said anything, either."

"Oh, he would have said. You should have heard the things he said about Angelo Gaja. He loved to talk about his fellow wine-makers. But, you know, there's a reason everyone is protecting this Scanavino. They must feel sorry for him."

The next morning was so clear that we could almost see Mont Blanc. We munched cookies all the way to Verona, where the weather was predictably wet and dreary. That night, for some fortuitous reason, we decided against heading to the legendary wine bar called Bottega del Vino in the center of town. I've spent some quality time there, evenings when old wines flowed like Pepsi does at a diner. At this Elaine's of the wine world, everyone showed up. Marvin Shanken, publisher of *Wine Spectator,* showed up. Right behind him, the chef Mario Battali, pushing his great girth around. The rooms are so crowded that there could be less than an inch of air in the entire place at three in the morning. Frankly, it's a hoot, and a great place to exercise one's flirting skills. Skinny and I had both enjoyed some memorable encounters there. But on this first night in Verona, we decided to save our energy for the exhausting days of walking and tasting VinItaly. We headed toward Il Carro Armato—"the Armored Truck"—a dingy wine bar with communal tables and a not-so-hot wine list on the fringe of the Verona action.

The list there is less inspired than the Bottega's: not a lot of old vintages, and few wines that I could even drink, but they did have one lonely bottle of a local, revered wine, a 1997 Quintarelli Valpolicella. Quintarelli has been a benchmark producer in the region for decades. Made from the classic grapes grown in Valpolicella, Corvina, Rondinella, and Molinara, Quintarelli is not made with *barriques;* instead, it is aged in large old Slavonian oak casks, so common all over northern Italy before the advent of the New Wine ways. The wine is much sought after, little is made, and at fifty euros it was on this list for less than what it would have cost retail in the States. *Yum.* My first glass was sparky, with nail-polish-removerlike acidity and gamey aromas. My nose was reaching for the next qualifier when restaurateur Joe Bastianich, chef Lidia's son, came floating in. Very much the impresario, he was followed by his entourage, trailing a respectful few meters behind him. Skinny jumped to her feet for a "kiss-kiss."

The donlike Bastianich, always gentlemanly and gracious, invited us to join them. We did, and brought our wine. Looking around the main room, with its picnic tables and benches, it was obvious: Our out-of-the-way Armored Truck of a wine bar had become the cooler Bottega.

Once we were seated, the Bastianich posse offered us their wine. Theirs were much more expensive picks. More expensive doesn't always mean better. This was one of those cases when it doesn't. I was *plotz*ing when Skinny gave them our decanter and tried not to show my despair when they emptied it. Skinny was so involved with all the male attention she was getting that she didn't even let on how horrible she found the wine they filled her glass with.

I was feeling bored and forlorn and, insult to injury, I had nothing to drink. Just when I was feeling like dog meat, I felt a tap on my shoulder. I threw my arms around the neck of Filippo Antonelli, one of the winemakers I like from Sagrantino's home town, Montefalco. Filippo introduced me to his friend, who in fact was the maker of Rocche Castlemagno, a Barolo I had drunk one night at Bottega's while happily flirting with a bearded, hippie-type man with a deep, sexy voice. The world of a wine writer is sometimes thrillingly small. When Filippo asked me to join them, I left Skinny and table hopped. At that moment, I was feeling quite at home. Taking in his tussle of brown curls and sensuous, fleshy earlobes, which looked so swollen that they might burst, I asked him, "Do you know a someone named Giovanni Scanavino?"

There in Verona, at this crowded wine bar, the man said yes.

I told him of my failed visit to Piedmont. I tried to make it sound as pathetic as possible. Taking pity on me, he told me what he knew. "There was some sort of scandal. Scanavino put some-thing bad in the wine. It was more that than bankruptcy. Maybe it was methanol. There was a rash of that sort of stuff in northern Italy in the late seventies and early eighties."

So much for getting a good night's sleep. When we walked back to the hotel, not long before dawn, I told Skinny about the latest development in the case. The plot thickened. I was getting close to solving the mystery. The maker of the wine that seduced me into this love affair with Barolo was unscrupulous!

"Oh, God. He killed someone!" Skinny cried out, and cupped her hand over her mouth.

That was a sobering thought. How awful. Could it be? Or maybe it was just as simple as putting some wine from the south into his Nebbiolo, some strong Primitivo to give his wine some backbone. There was a long historical prerogative here. Maybe his problem was that he, the poor *schnook,* got caught. Our imagina-tions ran away like wild horses into the sunset. Scanavino was in-deed a Scandalavino.

In the morning, we took our place among the battalions of merchants, journalists, winemakers, and wine buyers storming the gates. VinItaly is a huge show. Rollerblading might be the best way to get around. But we had our legs, so we sprinted through the rain and the pavilions, passed some of the silliest promotions I ever did see for wine—scantily clad, large-busted women pro-moting Pinot Grigio with facials and massage?—to pavilion 9, where the Piedmontese producers were housed.

We stumbled upon the stand of Eredi Lodali, a winery in the area of Treiso d'Alba, located down the road from that first young winemaker Elena wanted me to save. Walter Lodali, the heir apparent of the winery, poured us his 2001 Barbaresco. Skinny and I traded looks as if we had just seen the cutest puppy. The wine, she was good. The first wine of the day, and it was great. *An omen.* Now that he could see we were fans, he poured the 2003 and said, "Now you'll see a big change."

"Of course," I said. "It was the hot year. Nothing from 2003 tastes typical."

"Oh, yes, but you'll see something else."

One sweep of the glass past my nose told me everything I needed to know. The wine was stripped and sanitized. It was airbrushed. It was a tragedy. The 2003 vintage was hot and sunny. I wanted to smell it in the glass. But no. There was nothing to tell me a damned thing about that vintage. I wanted to weep. Skinny, too. I asked, just to make sure. Did he do a pre–cold soak for a long time? The answer was yes. Did he yeast for the first time? The answer was yes.

I don't know what else he did to the wine, but I really didn't care. If the wine had had a gorgeous Roman nose, it now had a snipped one. Then, as if we didn't have enough pain, Lodali said, "Since we have the consultant, the *Wine Spectator* asked us for samples!" He was so proud. My heart broke for him.

It was less innocent over at the Marco de Grazia booth. There, I was surprised to find many 2002 Barolos. When tasting at the Seghesio table, I asked why the winery had been able to make a

Barolo despite the weather that year. Their answer? There was nothing the matter with the 2002. That *might* have been the case for their particular vineyards, but it was unlikely. A more honest response would have been, "True, the vintage was difficult. But we were lucky. We weren't able to make as much Barolo as usual, but we had enough wonderful grapes to make some."

At de Grazia we tasted Seghesio (unyielding, grape tannin replaced by splinters), Moccagata (cough syrup), Scavino (burning rubber), and Bergandano (let's not go there). We saved the Cavallotto for last, because of the winemaker's reputation for standing up and saying *no* to the de Grazia "recipe." A Cavallotto was the first wine we'd requested at Le Torre when we were given that delightful Fontana instead. Yet, we found, Cavallotto was dead and alive at the same time. It was the *un*dead. How do they do that? At last, the Skinny Food Writer begged for mercy. "Not one more," she cried. "Please."

That night, Lars, our friend who worked for the Long Island/ Montalcino–based Castello Banfi, took us to a traditional restaurant where there were rolling carts carrying boiled cow heads, and other such treats. Trusting that most all the food would be drowned in animal caul, I went with a hunk of cheese and some salad, but had a great time watching Skinny chomp down on *nervetti,* chewy beef tendons, while we all washed the meal down with a pleasant lambrusco.

Because Lars works with Banfi, he couldn't go on record and agree that he, too, preferred the kinds of wines we did. But when he makes his own wine at home on Long Island, like my grandfather, he uses no additives, not even a splash of sulfur. His secret is a dash of Thompson seedless grapes.

He waited until his espresso came to bring us up-to-date. "I did a little snooping for you about Scanavino," he said. "My Barolo contact got back to me and said some local checking with his father and a friend of his father's confirms his disgrace seems to be more of a personal nature than a public-endangering Scandalavino—he sold off his family business in a bad deal for him and ended up with nothing. No money, no winery, no heritage, and you know in Italy, that's worse than killing somebody. Loss of *figura* is the deadliest shame."

Skinny and I were not convinced. We were still certain that Scanavino had killed someone.

This loss of *figura,* losing face, though, was worth considering. Not only did Scanavino lose *figura,* but so did all of Italy! Barolo, as Maria Teresa said, had a noble soul. Not only was it noble, but historically it was one of the world's most important wines, right up there with Burgundy and Bordeaux. With modern techniques Barolo loses its identity. The same is true of most Italian wines. Take the wines of Tuscany. How many Chiantis with individuality are left? What about the wines from Abruzzo or the wines from Campania? A few years ago I visited the winery Mustilli outside of Naples. The red grape they grow is Aglianico, and I tasted several vintages from the 1990s, wines redolent of licorice bark. Then we got to the 2001. The wine was flat. I asked what was different. The difference was the new wine consultant from Tuscany. Then a Merlot was poured. Why grow Merlot there in

Sant'Agata De Goti, where it is not indigenous? I asked. The daughter of the man who'd made the gorgeous wines before the consultant arrived told me, "To get the attention of journalists, we need to have a Merlot."

And now the spoofulated wines were all over VinItaly. When will Italy save face? When will they return their wines to the throne? I felt the Italian situation was almost as bad as the one in Rioja, until the next day, when Skinny and I played hooky from VinItaly and set out for ViniVeri. After the particularly depressing day we'd had, I couldn't wait.

Thanks to Skinny's brilliant way of communicating with strangers, whether she speaks their language or not, we arrived at an ivy-covered villa near the highway. With cars pulled up alongside the tree-lined road and the air smelling sweetly of early spring, the scene was a vivid contrast to the vast parking lots, buses, and mini-metropolis of VinItaly's pavilions. And inside, the show had the feel of a mild-mannered country wedding.

There were seventy-five exhibitors, we noted, almost half from Italy. *There was hope!* Might I one day be able to happily drink Italian wines again? Big Joe appeared as if sprung from a cloud, gave an air kiss and a slightly evil *heh-heh,* and then disappeared to taste with his flock.

Unlike gargantuan trade shows where the wineries have easy entry, having to do little more than send in an application with a large check, decorate their booth, and set up their bottles, ViniVeri requires exhibitors to share a winemaking philosophy and meet a certain level of quality. So my old standby question, whether a winemaker inoculates or not, was moot at this wonderful, wine-affirming affair.

I was eager to meet Paolo Gargano, the Genoa-based wine importer whose company, Triple A, had helped to organize this gathering. Flipping through the Triple A catalog, I saw many of Big Joe's wines. I also saw Triple A's manifesto, a multiple-point list of good and bad practices in the vineyard and winery. There were lots of *Nos*: No chemical farming. No enzymes. No bacteria to promote malolactic fermentation. No reverse-osmosis or concentrator machine. No micro-oxygenation. No added tannins or oak chips. No added grape must. No added acidity. No deacidification. No overt usage of new wood. Little or no use of sulfur.

Yes, it seemed, the Italian natural wine movement was coming up and gaining momentum.

When I met Paolo, he told me that he used to be more lenient about the winemakers he took on to distribute and import when he knew less about winemaking. "For example," he said, "I used to import the California wine Caymus. I dropped them because they used yeasts and god knows what else. They were furious."

I asked him if restaurants understood the kinds of wines he offered. Did they get the concept beyond the taste? I thought of my friend Elena, whose organic cooperative had been slow to gain the acceptance of her fellow Piedmontese, because organic and natural principles were viewed as crazy by some.

Restaurants, Paolo assured me, loved his wines. Yet, he confided, there were some uncomfortable incidents. Just as we have the Big Wine families Gallo and Bronco in America, many Italian wine lists and stores are dominated by Italy's own big family-owned wine companies. Some restaurateurs, after dropping those more conventional wines and choosing wines from Triple A instead, experienced threats—not to their kneecaps, but to their restaurants' reputations.

When we reached our tasting saturation point (a happy one), Skinny compared our numbers to those of the day before. At Vin-Italy, we'd tasted 104 wines, out of which we liked four. At Vini-Veri, we tasted sixty wines (in two and a half hours), liked about 90 percent, and loved about 70 percent. Not all were Italian but there were a lot more good Italian wines than I would have guessed.

In the car, Skinny wanted to know whether Paolo's restaurant story indicated that conventional wine producers were feeling threatened.

"I doubt it," I said. "Making wine in the international style has made people a lot of money. Anyway, salesmen strong-arm restaurants all the time, even in the States. European winemakers have more to worry about with the local bureaucracy.

"Get this story Big Joe told me. You know Silvio Montesecondo? His lovely Chianti producer? Joe visited in the spring of 2004 and tasted the 2003. The wine is a mix of Sangiovese and Canaiolo. It was still in the tank. Big Joe loved the wine as it was and found it juicy—not a term I usually hear him use, but what the hell, he is entitled to be out of character on occasion. More importantly, he thought it really tasted like Chianti. Joe encouraged Montesecondo to bottle it without putting the wine in barrels. Silvio wasn't sure he could make a wine without wood. That's when Joe opened up a cute little wine from northern Italy, a Ruché that had no wood influence. Silvio loved the wine and decided he would try the 2003 without wood.

"Well, the wines of both Silvio and his neighbor, the highly regarded Paolo di Marchi from Isole e Olena—who made a wine in the old-fashioned style—failed to get the DOC (Denominazione di Origine Controlatta) mark of approval. This meant they could not use the term *Chianti*. Instead, they had to use the far less prestigious *IGT* (Indicazione Geografica Tipica). The reason cited was lack of color! But they were told unofficially by a person of influence inside the chamber of commerce that if they added a color-fortifying agent the wines would pass!"

"Ick!" cried Skinny.

"Yes, *ick* indeed. But this is what we're up against in France and Italy and Spain. No one knows what authentic is anymore, even the people who are supposedly protecting the regional identities. It all went downhill when they made it legal to plant Syrah and Petite Verdot in Chianti and allowed Chardonnay in Rioja. The big wine company who got upset with Triple A doesn't like to lose their place on wine lists, yet they have little to worry about. I don't doubt the story one bit, but it sure seems petty."

On our way back to the hotel, we passed a striking poster. "Stop!" Skinny cried. She ran out of the car, and I took her picture in front of an angry red sign showing a pitchfork. Skinny raised a fist and smiled a huge one in front of the sign, which said, TERRE RIBELLI/CRITICAL WINE.

We took the sign as a sign. Optimistic about the future, not only of Barolo but of Italian wine in general, we prepared to leave Italy. I had to get back for Passover.

It was going to be a difficult switch from the spectacular wines of ViniVeri to the sad kosher wines I'd be drinking at the holiday. There has been *some* progress in the world of kosher wines, but not much. I had to find something drinkable to fortify myself at the seders, where drinking four (small) cups of wine is required.

For years, my mother was embarrassed that I was a wine writer. *This is what you do? This is what I sent you to yeshiva for?* But after shul that Passover, the rabbi spoke to me for the first time in twenty years. "So I hear you write about wine," he said. "Any recommendations?"

I wish I could have told him about some great kosher Barolo, but I've yet to come across one. I wish I could tell him about *any* great Italian kosher wine, but if there was a history of kosher wine in Italy it disappeared with the Nazis. I was able to tell him about a 2002 Abarbanel Riesling from Alsace, a bargain at eighteen dollars. And my mother got to be proud, having received a stamp of approval from this Orthodox rabbi, who left us saying something about finding me a husband.

Several months later, after the Jewish New Year, I was invited to take part in a panel discussion about Italian traditional vs. innovative wines in Los Angeles. I almost said no, until I saw that one of my fellow panelists was Luigi Bersano, the managing director of Mondo del Vino, the second buyer of the Scanavino company. Then I immediately said yes. In a conference room at the Four Seasons Hotel, I introduced myself to Bersano. He apologized for his English, which in fact was perfectly lovely. It didn't take two seconds for me to ask, "Did you know Scanavino?"

The smile faded from his lips. "I am very sorry to tell you, but he passed away a few weeks ago."

"Yes, I heard he was very ill." I didn't really have a strong reaction, because I had already given up on Scanavino. "But did you know him?" I pressed.

"Yes, I did know him."

It took a while for that one to sink in. I had asked so many people this question. I had come so close in Piedmont, but it was here, six thousand miles west, in Beverly Hills, where I found someone who knew the object of my obsession. A fervent jumper on hearing good news, I started to bounce. But seeing as I was to be on a panel in a few minutes and needed to hold on to a modicum of professionalism, I folded my arms in an attempt to restrain myself. "You really did?" I asked.

Signore Bersano surely thought I was nuts. He explained, "I used to sell his company sparkling wine to bottle. Yes. I knew him."

"Would you mind telling me something about him? Something personal?"

"Why do you want to know?" he asked kindly, if a bit suspiciously. I launched into my spiel. At this point I knew how ridiculous it sounded. I was probably the only one Scanavino had launched into a career of being nuts about wine.

"That is a very nice story," Bersano said. "There was a time he was known as a very good producer."

This was news to me, and I was feeling a little less ironic about my obsession, a little more vindicated.

"I will tell you about him. He was a very, very nice man. His family used to be in the chicken business. Scanavino used to call himself Polli. He used to say, 'I was born a *polli* and will die a *polli*,' and he didn't know how true that was."

My Scanavino had just gone from murderer to a poor lone chicken.

There was more. "I'll tell you one other thing," Bersano said. "Scanavino used to play medieval games. It is a big thing in Alba, it's sport. And he also sang, and he looked like me."

I looked at him quizzically. "Handsome like me, tall and handsome," Bersano explained. *And modest?* I thought. But it was obvious that Bersano was quite fond of Scanavino.

"What happened? Was he caught putting something in the wine?" I asked.

Bersano's tone became guarded. "Everyone back then did."

Yes. I remembered the conversation with Maria Teresa. So many people always ignored the laws and cheated. "The difference was, he got caught?" I asked.

He didn't say yes. He didn't say no. What he did say was very interesting nevertheless. "He loved land. He bought land. But he didn't realize how expensive it was to work the land. Then he had to sell it off. He might have put something into his wine."

At least the Scandalavino that Skinny and I had been so caught up in wasn't about a murderer. It was about a *polli*, a simple chicken man, who loved land. Out of sheer, random luck, from the hands of Madame Chauchat, a woman I couldn't stand, I was given the best wine that poor man had ever made. It was an old-fashioned Barolo, the color of caramel instead of purple passion. It was rosy and suedey, the wine that changed my life.

– 7 –

The Lone Guinea Fowl
of Burgundy

Around Labor Day in 2002 we were staying with my friend
Becky Wasserman at her fifteenth-century limestone farmhouse
in the miniature village of Bouilland, Burgundy. The weather had
turned dry from wet and was perfect for ripening the grapes. Each
night before sunset, the man I loved stepped into a field that sat
beneath alabaster cliffs, adjacent to the pasture land where ghostly
Charolais cows grazed, and hooted back at the owls. Becky was
charmed. Having a soft spot for lost boys, the way I do, she
understood him immediately, and affectionately named him the
Owl Man.

I have attachments to Burgundy. It is the only wine area where
he traveled with me. It was there I sensed that he would one day
leave me. And during that trip, I began to intuit that learning
about Burgundy could be more intimidating than reading
Finnegan's Wake.

Of the six areas of Burgundy, it is the Côte d'Or, made up of two lobes, the Côte de Beaune in the south and the Côte de Nuits in the north, that gets the Burgundy fanatic's attention. Burgundy is a crazy quilt of named vineyards. Among them are 465 premier-cru vineyards and 33 grand cru. Picture the appellation as a thirty-mile-long hero sandwich: the premier-cru vineyards are the two pieces of bread and the grand-cru vineyards form the stuffing. That "stuffing" is made up of highly protective microclimates and soil rich in fossil-laden limestone and with a composition so complex that it changes with every breath. You don't have to geek out about Burgundy to enjoy the wines, though enjoying the wines does—I'm sorry to confess—eventually tempt you to spend all of your disposable cash on them.

Though I was fortunate enough to cut my Burgundy teeth at Becky's table, for a long time something was missing from my Burgundy tastings: Never had I sipped a wine from the best domaine, from the finest part of the stuffing. I'd never had a transformative Domaine Romanée Conti experience—or for that matter, any DRC experience. Confessing to this lacuna in professional situations was embarrassing. I was like a travel writer who had not been to Paris, a food writer who had not experienced a white truffle. How had I missed this rite of passage with a wine that had the most mystique of all?

I knew the history. Domaine Romanée Conti is in the town of Vosne Romanée. The domaine only makes wine from grand-cru vineyards, two of which, La Tâche and Romanée Conti, are *monopoles*—the domaine owns them in their entirety. In 1562, the

Romanée St. Vivant monks identified the special wines derived from the Romanée Conti vineyard, at the time called Le Cloux des Cinq Journaux. When the vineyard was next sold, the new owners renamed the vineyard Romanée. The subsequent owner was a prince. Prince de Conti took possession in 1760. He found the wines so spectacular that he greedily decided to keep the entire production for himself. Then, after the revolution, the wealthy class, stinging from their losses, discovered the vineyard right next to Romanée, La Tâche, and that vineyard's reputation also grew.

After Prince Conti's death in exile, the vineyards were sequestered by the new state. When they came up for sale, it was under the name Romanée Conti. A couple of sales later, in the mid-1860s, the domaine fell into the hands of a Monsieur Duvault-Blochet, who was about eighty years old. He started to acquire the rest of the vineyard holdings, which formed the bulk of the current domaine. Duvault-Blochet's great-granddaughter married Gaudin de Villaine, who took the vines—which had fallen to shambles by 1911—seriously. The domaine started its second climb to greatness. Gaudin was the great-grandfather of Aubert de Villaine, the current co-manager of the domaine.

But does this convoluted history say a damn thing about why the wine is so great? Does it say anything about why, when asked, "Which Burgundy changed your life?" so many wine lovers whisper, "Domaine Romanée Conti," like Citizen Kane invoking Rosebud. Or else they burst into tears over the memory of La Tâche? Were these people just putting me on? Were they just recalling how much money it had cost them?

Hearing the answer DRC over and over again did not bore me—it made me envious. It was similar to when, at seventeen, I read *The Electric Kool-Aid Acid Test* and thought: *Me, too!* I want that hallucinogenic experience, too! And when I finally had my experience with hallucinogenics, the world forever looked different and I learned so much about life that—quite the opposite of regretting the experience—I am grateful. But a magic mushroom or hit of acid was a lot cheaper than a bottle of DRC, which went for five hundred bucks. So it was a long time before I could see for myself if DRC was Burgundian truth in a bottle, the *ne plus ultra* of the category. As I had always hoped, the opportunity did come and nothing kept me from it . . . unlike a certain friend of mine.

Now, I've done some stupid things in my life's battle for wine and love, but something the Skinny Food Writer did really took the cake. Instead of accompanying me to a thousand-dollar-a-plate dinner where Robert M. Parker, Jr., was guest speaker and where there would be more Domaine Romanée Conti flowing in one night than we would see in a lifetime, she went on a date.

"You'll regret this for the rest of your life," I warned her.

Her loss was Mr. Bow Tie's gain. This was in the beginning of a romance that blossomed from friendship, some months, perhaps too few, after my breakup with the Owl Man. At this point in our courtship, Mr. Bow Tie was a fan of California wine. He also preferred Great Western "Champagne" (the New York sparkler) to most French stuff and had only recently learned that Burgundy and Hearty Burgundy bear no relation to each other. But he was happy to fill Skinny's shoes. We stood cozily side by side when we checked in for the dinner, consumed by the initial flush of infatuation. I was a little thinner than usual, teetering on high heels in a flirty pink dress and feeling very fit alongside Mr. Bow Tie. We received our table number and I handed over the bottle I'd brought to share. At these dinners, the house supplies some wine but basically it is one huge BYOB affair. Plenty of collectors in attendance had ten-thousand-bottle cellars stocked with lots of the choice stuff. In these situations, I can't compete. I have about three hundred bottles, not in some special, temperature-controlled environment (okay, I removed the radiators in my apartment and keep the air conditioner set on economy during the summer), but on shelves in my living room, in crates under my bed, and in cubbyholes in the bedroom. I have no wine older than ten years and certainly no DRC. In other words, I had nothing of worth to share. So I went for a conversation-piece wine: I brought a twenty-dollar Pineau d'Aunis so geeky that I was sure no one had heard of it. My bottle was numbered and carried away by a sommelier. Mr. Bow Tie and I grabbed flutes of Salon Champagne (*"Hmm,"* he said. "This really is better than Great Western!"), and joined the meet and greet. At the center of a crowd of men in formal suits sat, as if on a throne, *the man,* my own personal Kurtz—Robert M. Parker, Jr. His hair was as matted as a Brillo pad. I had heard lots of rumors that his health was bad, that he had gout. I whispered to Mr. Bow Tie, "The man who is not welcome in Burgundy is honored tonight." Mr. Bow Tie asked, "Not welcome?"

I told him about "l'Affaire Faiveley." In the 1993 *Wine Buyer's Guide,* Parker ended a section on the Faiveley wines with these remarks: "Reports continue to circulate that Faiveley's wines tasted abroad are less rich than those tasted in the cellars—something I have noticed as well. Ummm . . . !" Faiveley sued Parker for libel in French court and won on the basis of that *Ummm*. The winemaker asked for one American dollar and a retraction. It was a matter of *figura,* as they say in Italy.

As much as many people didn't love the idea of Parker, the critic Rovani was a far more alienating critic. While Parker may not have understood how much Pinot Noir can change after bottling, as it is a supremely sensitive flower, Rovani just didn't seem to know Burgundy. I was just one of the many who disagreed with him. I told Mr. Bow Tie how, at a wine festival in Oregon, Rovani and I had a very public debate on the 1998 vintage, one he reviled and one I believed was beautiful because of the gorgeous tannins most wines had. Then I told Mr. Bow Tie about the funny blog by the owner of a New York City auction house and wine store, Acker, Merrall & Condit. John Kapon, the co-owner, posted his dinner conversation. At dinner were some pretty knowledgeable people. Paul Wasserman, my friend Becky's son, Allen Meadows, who publishes a prestigious wine newsletter called *The Burghound,* and Mr. Bernard Hervet, who at the time was managing director of Bouchard Père et Fils (and who by now, interestingly enough, had moved to Faiveley). He said that there was a huge debate about Rovani, how true Burgundy lovers paid little attention to Rovani unless they were looking for extracted wines high in alcohol, sugar, or oak, and how that type of wine was far from what most Burgundy lovers sought.

TAKING THIS ALL IN, Mr. Bow Tie encouraged me. "Go ahead," he said, scooting me in Parker's direction. "Go ahead, you be a good girl and go over and introduce yourself. Don't be shy. How many times have you interviewed him?" I had interviewed him quite a few times. Our first interaction involved a fax he sent me stating that the wine world is a better place because of him. But consequently, we'd had an extensive chat for a *New York Times* article, in which I broke the dramatic news that while other wine writers avoided coffee or garlic prior to wine tasting, Parker shunned watercress.

Oh, what to call him—Mr. Parker? I wondered as I moved in his direction. Bob, which is what everyone calls him, just sounded too familiar. I compromised. "Hello, Robert," I said, and started to reintroduce myself, but I didn't have to bother because he knew immediately who I was, or faked it excellently. He even said that he admired my work. He was likable. I didn't want to like him. Wanting to justify my anti–Parker stance, I had pinned all that was wrong with the wine world on him. Nevertheless, he had a charismatic quality that made everyone want to be his friend, and I, too, was charmed.

Mr. Bow Tie and I took our place at our table, where my Pineau was already waiting, along with the other bottles our tablemates had brought. The group of us began sharing several

Domaine Romanée Contis. Were they worth all the fuss? Let's just say that the 1987 DRC Le Montrachet was one of the giddiest white Burgundies ever to slide down my gullet. It had a riveting element of deep, blushed apricot, toffeed butterscotch, a finish that just kept going, and such a fresh acidity that I just had to keep on smiling. The oldest DRC I had that night was a 1966 Romanée Conti that came directly from the prestigious table where Parker sat. Pretty fascinating: A dash of Tabasco and red pepper, then it was all a tumble and jumble of allspice, nutmeg. It was like sticking my tongue inside a cinnamon stick.

We got to taste such great bottles because we were sitting at a table with a wine importer, chef Daniel Boulud himself, and a few sommeliers who knew every collector in the room. This is why, too, all of a sudden, Mr. Parker was over my right shoulder saying to Mr. Burgundy importer, "Funny, isn't it? The most hated man in Burgundy being the guest of honor?" Mr. Bow Tie thought I was a very talented girl, as if I had set Parker up to say such a thing. I admit, I was further charmed that Parker could be so light-hearted about the situation. In the midst of this tasting orgy, Mr. Bow Tie ran for his train at ten o'clock, which made me seriously ponder whether I could ever be in love with a man who walks out on DRC, even if he did smell like white truffles to me.

Newly deserted, I watched forlornly as my tablemates left to go hunting other goodies. But on the table to keep me company was another orphan, a magnum of 1989 DRC Grands Échézeaux. It wasn't La Tâche, but I was not going to hold that against it. I so wanted to plug it up and take it home with me. But I alternated drinking in its aroma with drinking the liquid until I was afraid I would be too tipsy to walk to the door without making a fool of myself. Falling on my ass is not the way I wanted to be remembered by Robert Parker or the other esteemed guest that night, Aubert de Villaine. Nope, when I visited M. de Villaine, co-owner and managing director of DRC in Burgundy, I wanted him to remember me as a girl who can hold her Grands Échézeaux.

SOON AFTER MY first DRC experience, I e-mailed Becky to tell her I was coming over for an appointment with Aubert at DRC and, bless her curly head, she said, Come, your bedroom is waiting.

Becky Wasserman moved to Burgundy in 1968 with her (then) husband. When he retreated to the States, Becky, having fallen for Burgundy in a big way, stayed on with her two sons and made her home the village of Bouilland (population 120, lots of white cows, and a few horses). Seeking a livelihood, she sold French oak barrels to the fledgling California wine industry. But soon she ditched the barrels and created Becky Wasserman Selections. She was one of the first women to crash through the wall around the male-dominated wine industry. She attributes the fineness of her palate to myopia, insisting that poor vision enhanced her senses of smell and taste. She also once told me that selling Burgundy required the zeal of a missionary, the stubbornness of a mule, and the ability to change clothes in a telephone booth.

At one time Becky and I toyed with the idea of writing her memoirs. During one of our taping sessions, she told me an affecting, love-at-first-sight story. When the diminutive Becky Wasserman first saw the towering hunk of a Scotsman named Russell Hone at a London wine tasting, she was so flustered she didn't know what to say except, "What a lovely shirt." Russell was so flustered that he went out to buy her an identical one and toted it around the next day hoping to bump into her at another wine event. Some years later, Russell showed up at Becky's Burgundy farmhouse with two suitcases and never left. Russell, you see, is a very smart fellow.

It was mid-January when I pulled onto the gravel patch that lies between their twin farmhouses. I love everything about the place. I love the biodynamic garden out back, I love the plum trees (from whose plums I made an excellent pie during the summer I visited with the Owl Man). I love the sound my car door makes swinging shut in the pristine air. I let myself in, and there in the kitchen, opposite the 1950s bikini-clad girl on the vintage advertisement for Bile Beans, Russell teetered on a stool, an apron secured around his generous girth. He pared potatoes over the sink, a glass of Muscadet at his wrist. Without any salutation, barely giving his cheek to me, he said, "Cauliflower and cheese. Will that do for you, madam? Put down your bags and get yourself a glass." When Russell is around I have a very, very good drinking partner.

I walked into the dining area, where Becky was jotting an e-mail on her laptop. She stubbed out her cigarette and came to greet me. Her silver hair was threaded with black and her smile fetchingly girlish. They sent me off to my room and when I emerged slightly refreshed, dinner was as it always was, busy, this time attended by some British wine merchants. Years ago, Becky decided that, with her busy entertainment calendar—often booked up to six nights a week—she was better off inviting her business associates and guests to her home. Over the past three decades, dinner at the Wasserman-Hone household, usually with Mr. Hone as head chef, has become one of the most coveted invitations in Burgundy. From the father of nouvelle cuisine, Michel Troigros, to Justice Sandra Day O'Conner, and yes, Robert Parker, they've all been here.

The cauliflower and cheese was delicious. I was filled in on Becky's son, who'd recently returned from America to join the French side of the business, and spearhead the renovations on the second farmhouse. Who was I dating? they wanted to know. Soon they were rooting for Mr. Bow Tie. "So he likes California wine, are you really going to hold that against him?" they counseled. They caught me up on their good friend Clive Coates, a well-known Burgundy wine critic from Britain who had published *The Vine,* a wine newsletter, until 2005. I can always count on the unedited Clive to say things like, "Mr. Parker hated the '93s. He's a complete idiot." He's mischievous but also so good-natured. Just take, for instance, the one morning he was faced with a corked bottle of Riesling. He sniffed, wrinkled his nose. "It's corked," he remarked, then, "Oh well," he said, and poured himself a full glass.

Clive knows the hundreds of vineyards of Burgundy the way I know the stalls at the New York City greenmarkets. It's nice when he's around, not only because I learn so much from him, but he, too, doesn't eat meat, so I don't feel like the lone oddball. For the record, however, he does make allowances for foie gras and hot dogs (not sausage, but American hot dogs).

After dinner, Becky lit up a cigarette and fluttered those long lashes of hers, asking, "Where are you off to in the morning?"

"To see Aubert," I proudly announced. Becky had been friends with Aubert de Villaine ever since she arrived on the Burgundy scene. Those were the pre-Parker years, and Burgundy and the wine world were innocent. Becky tells tales of picnics in La Tâche.

The next morning, I left Becky's house and headed for the most celebrated village in the Côte de Nuits, Vosne Romanée. With its six grand-cru vineyards—Romanée St. Vivant, La Grande Rue, La Romanée, Richebourg, La Tâche, and the teensiest of them all, Romanée Conti—Vosne is a status town. I had full confidence that I could find the domaine. I'd driven by in the past many times with Russell and Clive, and thought for sure I'd recognize it.

I didn't.

So I stopped someone on the street, who pointed over my left shoulder. I was right in front of the Burgundy-red iron gates.

Much is written about the aesthetic of Burgundy: riches hidden behind stark medieval walls. Somehow, the area has resisted the temptation to open Napa-style tourist temples and tasting rooms. Here, the vineyards themselves are the tourist attraction. In any weather or season, tourists can be seen having their picture taken at Romanée Conti. Funny, I can't imagine people wanting to take snapshots of themselves in front of Mondavi's Napa Valley To-Kalon vineyard.

The winemaker of DRC is Bernard Noblet, who succeeded his father. This generational link between winemakers is a stark contrast to the way the New World producers fire or hire winemakers as if they were donut makers, as if there was no connection between winemaker, vineyards, and wine. Take, for instance, the case of Heidi Peterson, who made America's cult cabernet Screaming Eagle. With the wine famous from its first vintage, a new owner came along, doubled the bottle price to five hundred dollars, dumped Heidi, and took on a Michel Rolland disciple. I was appalled by her dismissal. In the New World, everything is disposable. In France and Spain and Italy, at least where the wineries are still independently owned and run, sons and daughters often take over from the older generation, even if, as at DRC, the domaine belongs to someone else.

M. Aubert de Villaine, the owner and managing director of Domaine Romanée Conti, is a handsome man, tall and lean with the bushy eyebrows of a Russian aristocrat. When he married his wife, a Californian named Pamela, they bought property in the humble village of Bouzeron in southern Burgundy and started their own winery—A & P de Villaine. But DRC is an institution, and Aubert guards it accordingly. In his modest office, I informed Aubert why I'd come. "I am deeply concerned about the effect the *Wine Spectator* and Robert Parker have had on the wine world," I told him.

He was intrigued.

I went on. "Burgundy isn't as profoundly affected but, still, there are too many Burgundies with the heft and concentration of a cabernet, trying for that power and concentration of Bordeaux. There are so many Burgundies that want to taste like a California Pinot."

He shook his head. He knew that Parker had a tremendous impact on the wine world, he acknowledged, some of it positive. But in his life outside of Domaine Romanée Conti, Aubert is active in the Nicolas Joly fringe wine festival, Les Renaissance des Appelations, and is a great supporter of naturally made wine. While Aubert considers Parker a friend, he expressed some concerns about the absoluteness of Parker's opinions. This business of making wine to please one palate was terribly problematic, he said, adding, "But if Parker was in the middle, no one would read him."

Aubert wasn't as fond of Pierre Antoine Rovani, however. Even worse, to his mind, was past Burgundy reviewer for the *Wine Spectator* Per-Henrik Mansson. For a while, in fact, he didn't allow Per-Henrik Mansson into the domaine. Aubert couldn't remember the specifics of their conflict, but Becky could remember the attitude. Apparently, Per had been a crime reporter and he could take up a similar attitude when he wrote about wine.

I'm not above a little wine gossip. I love it. But I had very little time with Aubert, and there were more important issues to tackle, such as the Parker influence on oak, color, uniformity, and the many technological roads used to deliver these characteristics.

Since 1982, before the height of the Parker effect, DRC decided to switch to 100-percent new oak. Aubert's philosophy is to give every vintage a fresh start without any influence of past vintages. Yet, to prevent the wood from imprinting onto the wine, DRC used barrels with minimal toast—just the toast coming from the heat needed to bend the staves into place. Then the barrels are air-dried for three years to further reduce interference.

When I taste DRC wines in their youth, I feel the wood quite a bit. But I never smell or taste the egregious cherry vanilla or almond crunchiness of other wines. As I saw the night I nursed my own personal 1989 magnum, the wood eventually integrates seamlessly, proving to me that, all right, if it's used correctly, I can deal with new wood.

In lesser *terroir*, like his own vineyards in Bouzeron, Aubert uses bigger, older barrels. The point was that, whether in Vosne Romanée or Bouzeron, oak should be a silent partner, whereas Parker wants the oak to screech. "Parker, you know," I said, "is a tremendous advocate of toast." I read Aubert this quote from the August 2005 issue of *The Wine Advocate:* "I am a great believer that low yielding, highly concentrated Pinot Noir deserves plenty of toasty new oak."

Aubert, a defender of the concept of *terroir*, replied, "I'm in total disagreement with that, but I have never discussed this with him. Toast can erase the necessary transparency of the wine. This leads to a discussion on the meaning of *concentration*. With this word, I do not mean big, massive, opaque wines, but wines that focus on their true character, on what makes them different and exceptional.

"In my view," he continued, "with wine, anything that is worth doing is usually worth underdoing. Overdoing is the default of youth. Underdoing is the default of experience. More seriously, this overdoing which you, Alice, have noticed, is the visible side of what seems to me characteristic of the New World: the taste and search for recipes. You see it everywhere: the varietals that are chosen, all the same everywhere, i.e., the ones that command the highest value on the market—cabernet, pinot, etc. . . . because this is where the money is . . . All these things are directed to make wines that will sell more easily because they will appeal to what is called the 'taste of the consumer.' "

Eunice Fried—another writer who took refuge at Becky's when writing her book, *Burgundy* (1980)—quoted Aubert as saying:

> The major difference between the birth of wine in California and in our region is that we are living a creation that was begun hundreds of years ago without one bit of commercial necessity. In California commerce is behind every winery. The destiny of a region built with a necessity for profit will be different from the destiny of a region that began without a need for profit. Today you could not create Burgundy.

Aubert made our tour of the winery brief, stopping so we could taste some of the 2005 vintage, baby wines all, a mere five months old. About the Romanée St. Vivant, he said, "This wine is like my grandfather, it is insecure, it always looks for himself." When we tasted Romanée Conti, I perceived patchouli, exotic and green.

"Let's talk about that green," I suggested. "To me, it is salt on a tomato. It brings out the complexity." Aubert agreed, but he lamented, "Americans fear greenness—that, too, was Parker's doing."

Walking up to the vineyards would have been a treat, but the winter light was fast fading and so we drove. Most of the towns in the Côte de Nuits have a cluster of medieval buildings with a crosshatch of bucolic vineyards out back. The lanes are so narrow that only horses or bicycles seem worthy to navigate them. I liked being there in the winter, when it was scraped clean of the oeno-tourist.

Aubert's car came to a screeching halt when he saw an elderly woman walking on the narrow shoulder. She had regal posture. He ran out of the car, gave her kisses, talked with her excitedly, and embraced her with familiarity and warmth. He was smiling when he came back to the driver's seat. "That is Madeleine Noblet, do you know of her?" he asked, as if her name played big in New York City. "She is the domaine winemaker's mother. She was a remarkable vineyard worker. She took care of these vines." I had heard that pruning work is a highly skilled task, not easy. But I never quite understood that it was a *mètier* until I saw the respect on Aubert's face.

In moments, we were out of the car again looking at the vineyard that most view as mystical, the vineyard that has launched the palates of millions of wine lovers, La Tâche.

Clive Coates translates La Tâche to mean "the work," but according to my dictionary and all the cosmetic ads in France, *la tâche* means "the spot" or "the stain." Like all of the DRC vineyards, La Tâche has been worked organically since 1985. There have been some biodynamic experiments in the vineyard, but Aubert says he really doesn't see any difference. Many vignerons who go from organic to biodynamic say the same thing.

Aubert squinted in the late-afternoon sunlight. No one was working in the field at this late moment. He said, "This vineyard has talent and just needs room to express." He talked of La Tâche as if it were a gifted child who needed a very special kind of nurturing. He continued. "What is even more remarkable than its existence is that someone discovered it. Where is the beauty in land? It is not definable. It is either *terroir* or it is not. You can deny God if you wish, but not that the sun rises."

Narnia was shimmering outside my window when I woke up the next morning. The woodpile and the plum and walnut trees were draped in white. Pecking all by his lonesome in the yard was a guinea fowl. The night before, Becky, filled with compassion, had told me how the other chickens snubbed him. Her son Peter thought the solution was to put him in a pot. Wiser, Becky argued that all he needed was a mate. "There, there, Edgar," I'd told the bird. "Yes, sweetie, you need a mate, a nice Burgundy-loving mate, or are you just heartbroken? Some little chicken stole your heart or was wrenched from you for someone's pot, and you are in mourning." Even though Mr. Bow Tie was waiting in the wings, I felt a little bit like I imagined Edgar did.

WHEN I NEXT RETURNED to France, bud break was cresting all across the wine regions. Bud break marks the counting days for the harvest, which arrives about one hundred days later. Thousands of minute yellow-flower-flecked puffs filled the vineyards. A natural smell like Dove soap hung in the air. *Imagine that.* A smell I detested in real life was gorgeously sensual in its natural form.

I had written Becky that I wasn't in the best shape. I had probably picked up some nasty bug in Morocco, where I had been on assignment. I promised her—deeply hoping it was true—that I was not contagious but was definitely not well.

The Wasserman-Hone compound was silent when I arrived at six in the evening. I sat on the stone bench in the yard writing, my stomach starting to churn. I was just about to walk up the hill to the local hotel to beg the toilet when Becky and Russell pulled up. I am always hoping Russell will have lost some weight, but not so this time. He struggled to emerge from behind the steering wheel. Becky, on the other hand, had never looked better. She had pink cheeks—a clue she had stopped smoking. Instead of coming toward me, though, she walked sharply away. Then she turned around and frowned, or was that a scowl? She shook her finger. "You will not get me sick. Oh, no, not this weekend.

Now, stay far over there, and tell me, how do you feel, and how have you gone this long without a toilet?"

Becky could not afford to be sick because well over one hundred people were coming on Sunday for the annual ten-year anniversary tasting for the growers. This year we were tasting the 1996 vintage. Though Becky organizes it, hosts it, and does the invites, some refer to it as Clive's tasting because he historically has published his tasting notes.

Buttressed by Becky's acidophilus and charcoal pills, I practically slept for the next forty-eight hours, until Saturday, when sometime after midnight, Clive, barrel-chested in his shorts, *thrump*ed through my bedroom door, flipped on the light, and stared wildly at me in a state of fearful confusion. Then he realized his boo-boo and, with his tail between his legs, went next door to "Clive's Room."

In the morning, I nursed my coffee, the first I had been able to drink in days. I leaned against the kitchen wall, talking to Russell, already in a puddle of sweat as he poked cloves into an onion that was destined for a chicken and a pot.

Meanwhile, Becky was tidying. The heat of the day was menacing and Becky was fretting, yet her flowing linen shirt looked crisp and cool. She, like I, does not do well in the heat. We all remembered 2003, when we wilted in June.

"What can I do to help?" I asked Becky. Still babying me, she said, "You get out of the way. Go sit down with Clive and taste."

I felt like I had won the lottery. While I've drunk plenty a bottle with Mr. Coates, I've never joined him in such a formal tasting. From ten in the morning until four in the afternoon, we were supposed to taste 107 white and red Burgundies from the 1996 vintage. Twenty-five were grand cru from the area's best domaines.

I joined Clive in the living room. "Good morning, Clive. Sleep well?" I asked. We both started to chuckle.

"That was quite a fright you gave me last night," he said.

"Sorry about that," I said.

Then we dropped the embarrassment and turned our attention to tasting. Usually, when I sit down to taste I do it with no cere-mony. But Clive seemed to have a preparation ritual, and so I did as he did. I ceremoniously checked my glasses for off smells from the dishwasher. I ceremoniously tempered each glass with a little wine. Then I poured that wine into the next glass and then into the next glass, allowing the wine to absorb the smells until I finally dumped the dribble in the spit bucket. It was then that Clive con-fessed, "You know, sometimes I think I'm getting a little bored with all of this."

Bored with wine? Where was this coming from? Was this going to happen to me—one day I would be bored with wine? But then, my life was different. Though I was critical, I was not a critic. I didn't want to be a critic. I don't want to do as Parker was known to do, book a hotel room, line up the wines, and spit hun-dreds of times a day. Wine critics seem to have to assess wine as if they were looking at a musical score, without benefit of hear-ing the piece in all of its voices. I wanted the stories behind the wines, because they made them taste so much better. As Maria

Teresa had said in Piedmont, you should not take wine out of its culture.

But when the first bottles arrived, Clive's true feelings were exposed as he excitedly proclaimed, "And now we will see the truth."

We started with the Côte de Beaune, a region more known for its whites but with Volnay, Pommard, and Savigny can make fabulous reds as well. Clive likes to taste in silence, but I am prone to jabber. We compromised: I gave running commentary and he suffered. Three hours later, we had gotten through twenty-seven whites and twenty-three reds. The whites were pretty damn good. It had been a high-acid year, and many of them made my stomach gurgle and my teeth hurt, something that would have been remedied if we had been eating as well as drinking. The reds struck me as wildly different. The fruit was intense. Too intense. I was perplexed.

When we broke for lunch, Russell brought out Beaujolais, kicking off my favorite sitcom, *The Russell and Clive Show,* with Becky playing good-natured referee. Like so many old friendships, the men's seemed based more on irritation and one-upmanship than on any desire to listen to each other. Maybe this is why their interplay is so amusing for me: I grew up in a family where no one knew the first thing about listening. First Russell gave Clive crap for having supported the industrial wines of Georges Duboeuf. Then Clive chided Russell for liking Jadot's Beaujolais, which, in the end, we all agreed were oaked to death. But still, Russell won the popular vote because supporting

Duboeuf, with its hearty embrace of wine manipulation, was a big boo-boo.

Diplomatically, Becky changed the subject, and asked me, "Who are you visiting tomorrow?"

"Philippe Pacalet." *And they all moved away from me on the bench,* to quote Arlo Guthrie.

Clive searched his memory and then said, "A bad winemaker."

Mostly, Clive remembered him from Philippe's days as the winemaker at Prieuré-Roch. In the 1997 book *Côte d'Or,* Clive wrote, "Roch and his winemaker, Philippe Pacalet, operate out of a converted garage . . . Prices are very high here. But I find the wines slight and uninteresting."

By two o'clock we wrenched ourselves away from a (typically) terribly gossipy and congenial lunch, and went back to the salt mines. We had only two hours, and sixty wines in front of us, before the guests came. *Work, work, work.* Finally, we got to the grands crus of the Côte de Nuits, the part of Burgundy whose wines fanatics will give their first-borns for. Clive scanned the names of the wines up next, and his sleepy eyes opened wide. He clapped his hands, rubbed them together, and with the smile of a child about to get a big piece of pie, he rattled off the grands crus coming our way: "Musigny, Bonnes Mares, Richebourg. Aha! Now we're getting somewhere." Could this be the same man who just a few hours earlier had said he was getting bored with wine?

We plowed through more grands crus than I'd ever had at one sitting. While the pedigrees of the wines were incredible, I had the same feeling as I'd had earlier in the day—there was something very unbalanced about them. With a few notable exceptions, the fruit was almost as cloying as candy.

By four o'clock, the winemakers, guests, and anyone else who could secure a verbal invitation had arrived. Tuckered out from the tasting, I couldn't rally the needed belle quality for socializing. I sat under the tree in back of the house and talked with *Wine Spectator*'s Burgundy man, Bruce Sanderson. Bruce is an affable Canadian who veered from acting and modeling into wine criticism, and is generally viewed as one of the few on-staff men at the magazine with a sophisticated palate and not completely full of himself. Together we people watched. The chef David Bouley, who had driven down from Paris with his then-fiancée, stuffed himself on Russell's lentils and sausage and asked Becky, "What's good?" Among the vignerons were the LaFarge and the Seysses families. This was an afternoon of royals.

The last guest left at about eleven o'clock. Becky went off to bed. Around us were scattered tables, scores of purple-stained wine glasses, dirty plates, of the detritus of a hundred sated guests. I started to roll up my sleeves and clean. Russell intervened, saying, "It will be taken care of in the morning," and lit up. In the great see-saw of life, Becky had stopped smoking but Russell had started.

I sat down near him in front of the stone fireplace; I couldn't get the wines out of my mind. I needed counsel. "Russell," I began, "I want to talk to you about the wines. Increasingly, I find I have a very particular, peculiar palate and point of view. I often don't taste or see the world in the same way others do. Clive and

I disagreed on many of the wines. But then Clive and I have disagreed on Duboeuf as well as Philippe Pacalet—but on the whole, weren't those wines all fruit and acid? They were so damned fruity, there was no middle."

"Well, Alice, you see, there was a lot of new oak in 1996."

"Yes! There was. That's what I was thinking."

"What did you think of the Dujac?" he asked.

"I loved it."

"And the DRC?"

"Ditto, but way too young," I said. "Here's what I thought. Wines like Dujac and DRC were terrific because those domaines vinify with stems. Clive doesn't like the effect of stems, but I do. Without the earthiness from the stems, the wines were all fruit and acid. They didn't work. Destemming reminds me of the strange habit of peeling an apple or carrot, not eating the skin of a potato or cutting the bloom off of a Camembert. It reminds me of those who don't enjoy the smells of sex, and those who have to keep hand sanitizers in their pocket."

Russell slumped back into his chair with exhaustion, his eyelids fluttering down. Miraculously, instead of a snore, when his mouth opened words came out. "Well, you see, Mr. Parker (he said rolling the last *r* in a Northumbrian way) doesn't like stems, you see, they interfere with his color, you see, and so and so," he said, waving his cigarette for punctuation. The conversation was over. Russell, exhausted, had fallen asleep.

In theory and in print, Parker has denounced the use of stems—yet how to explain that some of his favorites actually use plenty? DRC, Leroy, Ponsot, these are all producers who use stems. Tiptoeing so as not to disturb Russell, I went into the study to steal some minutes on the computer. I jotted an e-mail to Allen Meadows, who, in 2000, ditched his investment banking life to start *The Burghound* newsletter. *Tell me about 1996,* I typed. *I only liked the wines with stems and destemming has caught on as the fashion. Could you please, please, tell me what's going on?*

In the morning, a very interesting answer arrived in my in box. Meadows knew exactly what was going on. He explained that stems release potassium, a base that lowers acidity. In the high-acid year of 1996, the stems helped to give the wines balance. Then he told me that certain critics—

That's as far as I'll go, I will not name names—gave out high scores for deeply fruity and powerfully colored wines. But nothing happens in isolation. Consider how a few historical events converged which popularized destemming. The superstar winemaker Henri Jayer, who was vociferous against "unripe stems," and made a fruit-forward wine, might have popularized the trend. There is also a financial advantage to destemming, which comes from the ability to crop at higher levels than you can if you include stems. The reason is, stems bring yet another source of tannins. Because Pinot is a thin-skinned grape with limited natural tannins resident in the skins and seeds, it's necessary to be careful about these other sources of tannins, which can of course include stems and barrels.

The only way to balance out another source of tannins, particularly what can be herbaceous tannins, is to reduce yields. And yield in Burgundy, in fact, in winemaking in general, is by far the most expensive aspect of wine and dwarfs by comparison the cost of new barrels or fancy equipment. This is why destemming was instantly popular—the Burgundians realized right away that they could raise yields if they destemmed, plus they had the wherewithal to do it with the advent of more sophisticated, and cheaper, crushers/stemmers.

I was still thinking of stems the next day. The vilification of stems helped to rob Burgundy of its ruby color and turned it as dense and dark as Cabernet. Add to that the toasty new wood that Parker loved so much, and a whole different style of Burgundy—which bored me—emerged, even from conscientious producers. Thankfully, even though Parker thinks Pinot "deserves copious amounts of toasty new oak" and believes in destemming, some of his favorite wines are made without "benefit" of either technique. Nothing is simple, is it? I was still churning through the whole situation as I reached Pacalet that day.

I found Philippe Pacalet working down in the cellar, bent over a barrel, his wavy hair suspended like a cloud. Everything about him seemed unstudied. Now, some cellars get me excited. With its yeast-covered old barrels—between five and seven years old—walls weepy with moisture, and its healthy smell of mushroom and forest, Pacalet's was one of them. By the light of a bare bulb, Philippe talked to me as he racked the wine, shifting the contents from one barrel to the next. He said he made wine like his grandfather did, but with more consciousness. I'm sure the fact that his uncle is Marcel Lapierre, the "no sulfur" guru in Beaujolais, also adds to his wine-making savoir faire.

He took a break from racking to give me some tastes. The wines didn't have huge color or density. They had delicacy and uncommon purity. I wonder whether they are as long lived as I would like them to be, but while they are with us in this world, they are zapped with vitality.

As he dribbled some Pommard into my glass I asked Philippe what he thought of the biodynamists. That got him going.

"The problem with Steiner is that he didn't drink!" he exclaimed, referring to the founder of biodynamics, Rudolph Steiner. "Steiner wants to show you who you are. Do you need a book every day to show you how to feel something? Can you learn from a book how to feel? You need to be artistic, not monastic, and Steiner is monastic."

Pacalet also firmly believed that, as man is made of minerals, so is grape. My UC Davis scientists might argue that, actually, we are made of water, and so is grape, but wine's expression of mineral is so much more interesting. My friends would laugh quite hard if they saw how often a winemaker plops a stone from his vineyard into the palm of his hand, stretches it under my nose, and says, "Give it a lick," so I can taste their *terroir*. There is something to be learned from these exercises but, I admit, not much. They are more silly than illuminating. In Philippe's cellar I tasted real *terroir*—tremendous differences in the way each plot of vineyard expressed itself. I didn't have to lick the earth. The taste was where it should be, in the glass.

All the wines we tasted were red Burgundy from different villages and vineyards, and they all had something different to say.

The Pommard was silky with lots of Chanel No.-5-ish powdery, rosy aromas and flavors. His Beaune had a touch of orange juice and black tea. His Ruchottes-Chambertin was built and corseted, all structure and flowers.

"You cannot talk about *terroir* if you use yeasts or clones," Philippe continued. "You cannot talk about *terroir* if you use new oak. It is too sweet, it adds the wrong sensuality to the wine." Sure, he was preaching to the choir, but nevertheless, this was the first time I ever perceived *terroir* so profoundly. The difference I saw in the glass is the difference the soil makes.

It was time to get back out into the heat of the day, away from the beautiful coolness of his weepy, chilly winery. My eyes took quite a while to get used to the brilliant Beaune light. Soon, I was with Philippe in his Jeep, heading to see his vineyards. On the way, I told him about the tasting at Becky's and how confused I was with those wines from the 1996 vintage. He confirmed what Meadows had told me. More winemakers in Burgundy had become suspicious about the use of stems. For someone who rejects Steiner, Philippe surprised me with his almost Jungian philosophy when it came to stems. "Stems are the masculine to the fruit's feminine. It is wrong to disturb the masculine and feminine order."

I'd like to see how his kind of philosophical thinking would fly at UC Davis. But to hell with the sexual balance of things. I just thought that wines made with stems often tasted better and aged more gracefully.

Philippe went on, reinforcing what I had already learned. "They absorb the color," he said, "which is problematic because people like Parker love a deep color and extraction. They are also important from a wine-making point of view, as they absorb alcohol and are a natural control for temperature. Now you know the secret of stems!"

Philippe is so quoteworthy and unselfconscious; he was made for the media, yet no one knows who he is. "Do you ever get frustrated by your anonymity?" I asked. After all, he has a family, a wife and four children, and he looks like a total schlep and is probably just schlepping along, just about making a living.

"I don't want my picture with Robert Parker in a magazine," he told me. "In Burgundy, people talk. It's best people don't know too much about you."

It was then that I started to look at him a little bit differently, not so much like Arlo Guthrie, but more like the lone guinea fowl pecking solo at the snow on Becky's woodpile.

Few people in Burgundy make wine as natural as Philippe's. When I asked him why more people don't know about him, he said, as if telling me the ultimate secret, about stems, about Burgundy, about the world, "The real thing is disturbing. Being authentic disturbs people."

– 8 –

My Date with Bob

When it was time to contact Mr. Parker, I had a feeling that a key to our differences lay in the debate about the word *traditional*. To make sure I knew what that simple word meant, I pulled out the dictionary.

Tradition: 1. The handing down of statements and beliefs from generation to generation especially by word of mouth.

There you go. Tradition refers back to the wisdom of the grandfathers. I should have looked at the dictionary sooner. This would have been fine ammunition when I talked to both Big Joe and Clark Smith. The problem wasn't with the word *tradition* itself; it was that the classic definition of *tradition* was forgotten.

I shot off my request to Parker. Would he receive me in person or, at the very least, on the phone? We could kick off the conversation with his concept of tradition and then, most importantly, I would get his take on whether the wine world was becoming standardized.

One morning I had my answer.

Dear Alice,

It sounds like you have been brainwashed by the disingenuous movie "Mondovino." If you have already made up your mind about this (à la Jonathan Nossiter), there is little reason for us to speak. But if not, I would love to talk via the phone, as the diversity of styles as well as the reclaiming of indigenous varietals has increased twenty- to one hundred-fold, offering just two reasons why I believe the opposite of your theme about standardization.

Let my office know if you would like to set up a telephone conversation over the next few weeks.

All the best,
Bob

I stared at the screen for a few seconds, waiting for the happy news to sink in that Parker had agreed to an interview. Now, I would have preferred Mr. Parker in situ, in his Parkton, Maryland home, but nevertheless I quickly called his office to snare that phone appointment before he changed his mind.

Even though he might be *"A grand, ungodly, god-like man,"* I was not Ishmael, and Parker wasn't Ahab. Neither one of us was Moby.

As I compiled my agenda for the Feiring/Parker telephone interview, I tried to articulate what I hoped to gain from our conversation. I wished for a dialogue as well as understanding. After all, I had interviewed him before, and there had been that pleasant meeting before the Domaine Romanée Conti dinner, where I found him a warm, personable man. I wanted to find out where and how we differed. I wondered if I'd be able to pinpoint his blind spots. Would I find out why he so loved toasty new oak? Was there a link to junk food? On a deeper level, I wanted to discover how it was that he and I, who worked in such similar worlds, had such dissimilar palates. A great example is a 2002 Bond Vecina, a Napa Cabernet Parker oozed over, giving the wine 95 points: "A primordial, tannic beast with a beef blood-like concentration, a huge, opaque purple color, and notes of scorched earth, blackberries, chocolate, camphor, roasted meats, and cassis. It's as if I took an aged porterhouse steak from Peter Lugar's famed restaurant, put it in a Cuisinart, and aged it in new French oak." That is a great description of a wine I would be quick to pour down the drain. It wasn't that Mr. Parker and I never overlapped on wine. As with art and music, there are pieces of aesthetic truth that just *are*. Even if you hate Dylan how can you not be moved by "Boots of Spanish Leather"? Is it possible to stand in the Florence Accademia and not be mesmerized by the hands of Michelangelo's *David*? Some of the overlapping wine truths for us were the undeniability of Chave's Hermitage and the Domaine la Romanée Conti La Tâche. Yet he loves the big Barossa Shirazes, and I love so many red wines from the Loire that he could never ever enjoy. I have close friends with different politics, yet somehow, different palates seemed a greater barrier to overcome.

Excited to hear about the upcoming telephone call, the Skinny Food Writer asked me to pose a question for her. "Find out if he thinks there is room in the critical world for other opinions."

I had to write the question down to make sure I phrased it correctly. It's not one that resonated with me but she's a smart cookie, so I promised.

The morning of our date it occurred to me to get dressed for the phone interview, but I couldn't find the time. Wearing one of my favorite sleep shifts, with demure lace in strategic spots, I placed the call. His assistant was surprised and embarrassed. "Did you really have an appointment?"

"Yes."

It wasn't written down on his calendar, and he wasn't there. Would I call tomorrow? Same time?

In the end it worked out, because when we finally connected he was apologetic and quite friendly. "It is totally my fault," he said. "I don't want to bore you with the chaos that is reigning over my universe." I did want to know about it, actually, but instead he launched us into the interview by congenially saying, "Hopefully I can convince you that the wine world isn't going crazy for one taste or bland flavors." Then he started to riff on his definition of *traditional*.

"You have to consider the great historic wines." He lectured me in an avuncular manner. "They are the benchmarks. Cabernet from Bordeaux, Pinot from Burgundy. In Italy it's Nebbiolo from Piedmont and Sangiovese from Tuscany. Historic reference points—those are the traditional wines." He went on to emphasize that benchmark wines meant wines made from the traditional grapes in the area.

So, I thought, this is why he had no compunction about giving high marks to a wine with no sense of place. This is why he could describe a Rioja as tasting like a Napa Cabernet and give it a stellar grade. Benchmark meant museum piece.

Sensing that I was flummoxed, he explained, "Styles in wine always change."

Yes. There we agreed. Style was fluid; bell bottoms one day, stovepipes the next. What was in style today—big, fat wines with gobs of fruit and clunk—could morph into a new taste for silkier, elegant wines tomorrow.

"*Terroir* is important. You can't make great wine in the Sahara. But let's not get carried away. How much is the land, and how much is imparted by humans, like commercial yeast or the choice of wood?"

These were excellent questions, ones I ask myself. When the human touch is felt in a way that obscures the *terroir,* that is where I draw the line. But I kept these thoughts to myself.

"People," he continued, "say all the time there should be transparency in wine. I don't know what *transparency* means. In a blind tasting I can tell the grape—you can taste a Bordeaux from a Pinot Noir, but a piece of land? I've never seen anyone do that."

Did he doubt someone could blind taste a wine? After all, it was rumored that he himself was a talented blind taster. I pondered. Abilities differ, but there's so much to be learned through the terrific party game of blind tasting. I love the blind-test game, especially as a game of flirtation. Once, a man I had a brief infatuation with challenged me to a game of wine dare. Such fun. He came over with a brown-bagged wine and poured me a glass. Hmm. It was thick. It was somewhat New World, but it could have been the vintage. I sensed Pinot Noir, but it was definitely Burgundy. There was a vein of rose in it. Definitely Côte de Nuits. I closed my eyes and channeled. "Chambolle-Musigny?" I asked? *Bingo.* I was unable to get the actual vineyard. Was it La Fuées? Les Amoureuses? While I've seen people who drink lots of Chambolle able to pinpoint a vineyard, that kind of detail was beyond my wine language. Perhaps that's what Parker meant.

Parker went on to defend the use of new, small, oak *barriques* as more important than *terroir.* "Domaine Romanée Conti is the holy grail for *terroir*-based Burgundies," he said. As his example he chose La Tâche, made entirely by one winery. "I think the vineyard La Tâche has an extraordinary character. You get used to it, and you can recognize it. Now that gets 100 percent new oak. Take that oak away and what would that wine taste like? I mean, would the La Tâche character come through? We don't know because they don't do it."

I wondered if I should tell him that, before 1982, DRC didn't use new oak yet the reputation of the wines was just as profound? Should I remind him that Aubert considers toast anathema?

Citing Guigal, one of his favorite producers in the Rhône, Parker went further. "Marcel Guigal pushes the limits on new oaks to forty-two months no matter what the vintage on his luxury cuvées. My wife has said to me, 'These aren't as good as you say, they're indeed too oaky.' For three or four years they are too oaky, but then the oak gets absorbed, leaving a subtle mocha or espresso note, leaving the fruit and the character of Côte-Rotie that dominates. It's like a chef making great reduction sauce."

It struck me that he tastes wine very differently from his wife. I also noted that he used similar terminology to Clark Smith's in talking about making wine, and also similar to that of the poor Paso Robles winemaker who spoke of making wine "soup." *Should I tell him,* I wondered, *that I don't want a reduction sauce in wine? Tell him I don't want my wine to* absorb, *I want it to* express?

"Most top winemakers are always trying to improve and make wine in the most natural, unmanipulated way possible." He persisted. "Wine is made more naturally today. Fruit is being handled more naturally today." He was trying to educate me, not seeming to grasp that handling fruit well had nothing to do with natural winemaking. "When I started out," he said, "I don't remember running into organically or biodynamically run vineyards. So the idea that you think there is a bland international taste out there . . . You can drive an eighteen-wheel truck through that argument."

I was tempted to climb into that eighteen-wheeler and turn the ignition. Natural handling of grapes? The Robert Hall Winery Web site claimed, "All grapes are hand-harvested in small, select lots. Fruit is handled as little as possible and each barrel is constantly monitored." Lot of good that did the poor wine. And so much talk about farming getting "greener" amounts to a bunch of buzzwords that mean nothing about the way the wine is made—"greener" practices in the fields have no connection with the way a winemaker processes grapes into wine. Natural handling, organic farming, and authentic wines are often unrelated. Even within the wine world it is debated how natural is natural. All agree the bare minimum is to start as organically as possible, and then: no inoculations, no additives, no flavorants (including oak), no use of machines to change the texture or flavor or alcohol level. Is it possible that the scope of possible wine manipulation had escaped Parker's vision?

One of his self-proclaimed contributions to the wine world was encouraging winemakers not to filter their wine. He most often links his definition of a "natural" wine to wine that is unfiltered. He believes that filtering strips wine of complexity. Filtering can indeed be bad for wines, but most excellent winemakers I've talked to agree that at times a light filter is necessary. And though Parker might punish a winemaker who filters with loss of points, he has never come out against the use of reverse-osmosis machines—what is that if not ultrafiltration? He has actually come out in favor of the use of the machines in Bordeaux, and his good friend, the flying winemaker Michel Rolland, is a huge fan of micro-oxygenation. Parker has given some very high scores to wines that have undergone this process.

At this point in the conversation, Parker's occupational hazard started to crystallize for me. According to the chief wine critic of the *New York Times*, Eric Asimov, Parker tastes up to ten thousand wines a year for evaluation. As a critic Parker focuses on wine tasting and scoring. His criteria, it seems, are power, concentration, and jam. He *quantifies*. As a writer, I focus on the way wine is made and why the wines I like taste the way they do. I focus on the story. I *qualify*. I am short. He is tall. I am urban; he is rural. I am left leaning; he swerves to the right. We were looking at the wine world from different points of view.

By this time I began to put more faith in Skinny's persnickety question. Ignoring my inner dread of it, I asked, "Is there room for other critical opinions?"

And that's where everything went wrong. "You know, I should be insulted," Parker said.

"Oh, now, please don't." I cajoled him sweetly yet with a painful awareness of how clumsy it all sounded.

"I have always believed in diversity of opinion," he recited, as if he had gone through this speech oh-so-many times. "I mean, I never commented on that woman's book [Elin McCoy's Parker biography, *The Emperor of Wine*], but the one real annoying thing—that was totally untrue—she said about me is that I have thin skin, that I don't accept criticism, and I go after wine writers. When I started out in 1978, I was very critical of others because, back then, like travel writers, most wine writers existed on the largesse of the industry. The British were the worst. Yes, there's plenty of room for other opinions. I just offer mine and try to do a good job, and hope most people agree."

"Obviously, they do," I assured him. "But perhaps you are misunderstood because you write with such an absolute conviction of being correct."

"It's a writing style," he admitted, calming down a little. "Maybe it's my training as a lawyer and preparing advocacy briefs. I do push it. People always come up to me and say, 'Gee, you're so different in writing than in person.' But when people call me a 'dictator,' it's about one of the most specious accusations that can be made about me. I am one of the most tolerant and open-minded people out there. I believe in wine diversity. And I'm there to protect it."

A few weeks later, I saw that Skinny's question had been prophetic. The Robert Parker universe had become a Mad Hatter party, and it was quite a puzzle to figure out what was going on. Rumors were flying like crazy that Parker had tried to hire Michel Bettane, his equivalent in France, to join his empire. Prominent others were supposedly approached as well. In the end, Pierre Antoine Rovani was out. David Schildknecht, an ex–wine importer, was in. The Italian wine reviewer Daniel Thomases was out. Antonio Galloni, who published a wine newsletter called *The Piedmont Report,* was in. Even though the review came from *The Piedmont Report* and not from *The Wine Advocate,* the erobertparker.com database shows a 94-point Lopez de Heredia white Rioja, a wine Parker had said he would never review because he didn't need any more enemies. And Schildknecht? He was respected. Becky referred to him as "a honey." In the August 2007 *Advocate,* Schildknecht posted his first Loire reviews and gave many Cabernet Francs high scores. One of Big Joe's wines, the Clos Rougeard Cabernet Franc, was knighted with 94–95. It is very possible that the new appointees could broaden or actually devalue the meaning of those points. The schizoid opinions of these diverse palates could well push many Parkerphiles to Paxil as they angsted over a deep identity crisis. Were they supposed to like these wines or not?

After a momentary chuckle, I had a stronger reaction—*Oh, shit, can't Bob wait for my book to come out?* After all, Rovani, with his Parkeresque disdain for red Loire wine, his lack of understanding of Burgundy, and his arrogant tone was such an easy target for me! Perhaps Parker himself was now saving the world from Parkerization. Maybe the wine world didn't need my help after all.

I definitely had to speak with Bob again. This time, for our morning interview, I got dressed—no more sloppy writer's habits for me. I wore full regalia—underwear, skirt, and blouse—and not only did I brush my teeth but I put on lipstick. I was prepared.

Our connection was off from the start. First, Parker was there to receive my call, so I didn't have the advantage of his being apologetic. In fact, he was defensive. I was paranoid. Had he Googled me? Had he discovered my anti-Parker tendency? Was Mercury in retrograde? This was a totally different Bob.

I started out applauding his new appointees to *The Wine Advocate* and suggested that he was embracing a more "global" palate.

"That's an absurd comment, an absurd comment," he repeated, peevishly going on to defend himself from this perceived affront. "I have a public forum on erobertparker.com embracing all points of view. You should call Pierre. Not once in ten years did I edit anything he wrote."

I suppose so, but not mine. I was kicked off in July 2007, a year after this conversation when the man who runs erobertparker .com, Mark Squires, gave me the boot from the site because I voiced a dissenting opinion.

"Wait, you're really misunderstanding me," I pleaded, breaking in attempting to explain my use of the term *global palate*. "Bob, now, you have a famous dislike for Cabernet Franc. David likes them."

"I like Cabernet Franc when it's good," he said. "I don't like them when they taste like V8 juice. I like the 1990 vintage last time I was in Troisgros, I drank a 1990 Jouguet Chinon."

That was just too nuts. It was 2006. In sixteen years the only other Loire Cabernet Franc he could applaud was a 1995 Domaine Alliet with a "a nice wallop of toasty, smoky new oak (the wine spent one year in 50% new oak barrels). This is a gorgeous, rich, un-Chinon-like wine . . ." It was a little bit like saying, *Some of my best friends are Jewish.* And 1990 was a very ripe year, very Californian. I asked whether he ever appreciated more delicate wines—or was his applause reserved for those over-the-top, jammy, oaky red wines. He answered by telling me that Chenin Blanc was the most underrated wine and he really liked Albarino.

Um, Bob? I was screaming inside. *Those are white wines.* Was this his way of avoiding giving me an answer that supports the evidence that those more delicate red wines don't register with him?

But I still wanted to get him to comment on reds, so I shot out a pointed question. "What about Gamay?"

"When it gets ripe," he said.

Like, Gamay has a hard time getting ripe these days? What was he saying? He liked Gamay only if it tasted like Merlot? Finally he said to me with a kind of pity in his voice, "I suspect you're one who doesn't like these big Barossa Australia Shirazes."

His annoyance was full-bore as he tried again to explain himself. "You know," he said, "I actually just write and take notes."

This was getting ridiculous. Parker can protest, jump up and down, chew tobacco, and wear overalls but he is not just some schlep from Parkton, Maryland, who scribbles noninfluential wine notes. "Come on, Bob," I said. "You're bigger than yourself. You can't deny that you've become an icon!"

"It might be hard for you to understand this," he answered, "and I don't care about that. I never really embraced it [the fame]. If I went from whatever position I have—which is embellished by other people—to anonymous tomorrow, it wouldn't bother me one bit. I am doing what I love, yes; I've become rich because of it. When my wife and I started out, I just wanted to make enough money to pay the bills. The problem is that you probably travel in circles where you can't have a wine conversation where my name doesn't come up. Myths about me get embellished, exaggerated. I have sixty-five thousand subscribers, but the *Wine Spectator* has what, four-hundred thousand? You're picking the wrong target here!"

I've never doubted for a second how much Robert Parker loves his mission, his job, or wine. I've never once doubted his sincerity. He was wrong, however, in his belief that his name came up in every one of my wine conversations. His name didn't often come up, *except* when I was on the job, visiting wine-makers. The winemakers were the ones who started that conversation, who invoked his name, who asked me whether Parker would like their wine, whether he would like the wine's color and power. That's because, from about the late 1980s onward, the Parker palate has largely dictated how wine is made world-wide. For the time being, when it comes to wine, *Parker* means power.

Parker was *not* Ahab. He was more like Moses. Being wiser than other men, Moses was held to a higher standard. Being wiser and purer than the *Wine Spectator* (*The Wine Advocate* does not take advertising), Parker should be held to a higher standard as well. If Parker wanted to, he could stop scoring, and make his readers and worshippers—and those marketers—read. Whether he intends it or not, thousands of wine shops and wine lists world-wide use his scores as promotional tools and people shop based on his numbers. Period.

He fought back. "You're holding it against me that people go into wine shops, if in fact they do, and ask for a *Spectator* or a Parker 90," he said. "Don't shortchange the consumer; they know when a chicken is a bad one or a good one," he asserted. "There is no global palate."

I was pacing back and forth in my desperation to find out what the source of the problem was. Outside, the city was tearing up my street, repaving. I closed the window, hoping for some quiet so I could think. It worked. I realized: I had used the word *global* and he, having taken such guff for the one-world, one-taste wines that had proliferated, was on hair-trigger defense. Not wanting to tell him once again that he misunderstood me, I adjusted my word choice. "Is there a mass palate?" I asked.

He said, "Well, for people who like Yellow Tail. But that's not the kind of wine any of us review." (I couldn't break it to him that he had given that Australian wine an 87 and some kind words. Not bad for a five-dollar wine.)

I was almost finished. I didn't see any way to salvage the interview; it had taken an unfortunate turn. There had been many such turns in the early days of my relationship with the Owl Man. Oh, I remember that struggle to communicate. Before love and understanding took over, he misunderstood me in every way. When he was in a certain mood, he held me accountable for every word. If we had still been together, would I have been more careful with my language during my conversation with Bob? Would I have used those verbal triggers *international* and *global*?

I found myself apologizing for the sloppiness of my interview.

"It just doesn't make sense," Parker told me. "No one in the history of wine has done more for the small artisanal producer— the kind of people you claim you like—than I have. You're trying to paint me [as] a big globalist, a tyrant, and a dictator."

I certainly did not mean to imply that he was. In the Hollywood version of the book, sure, the world's greatest wine critic would be in cahoots with the global companies, but not in real life. In real life Parker was a wine hero who had unwittingly unleashed an oak-and-technology monster on his favorite beverage of pleasure. Yet, something about being told what I was "doing here," made me more assertive. "My problem isn't with you," I told him, "but with producers and marketers who court your palate and change their ways because getting that score is so important."

Parker was disgusted with me once again. "I hear that people make wine for me all of the time. It's like the Spanish Inquisition—no one ever provides names."

"No? Well, I can provide you with some names." I told him that, when I visited winemakers from Croatia to Cahors, people asked me, What will Parker think of this wine? What will he think of this color? I've even been asked whether I could get Parker to visit them! "And I have to think," I said, feeling a bit like some inspirational speaker, gaining in strength and confidence as I went on, "*What did you do to get that color?* Those winemakers had a color in mind and went on the path to get it that way, instead of presenting a wine that is authentic, just because they hope to get your attention. You have nothing to do with the way they were trying to please you, but yet they did and they do."

What I didn't add is that with great power comes great responsibility. *That I look to you, Moses, to stop this craziness. I look to you, the one with power, to come out strongly in support of naturally made wines and to understand them.* I wanted him to embrace his power and use it for the good of the wine world. I couldn't stop him from loving wines that I hated—there should be room for all sorts of wines, the spoofulated ones as well as the real, the huge and the gentle. *But just know the difference!* I wanted to drop to my knees and plead.

Any time there are influential rankings—no matter what the industry—the industry will play to the scores. This is what I wished I could say:

Dear Mr. Parker,

Please do not continue to contribute to the dumbing down of the wine world. And if my Loire Valley Cabernet or Côt or Pineau d'aunis or Gamay start tasting like those Barossa Valley Shirazes, I'll have to switch over to calvados. Not that I have anything against a good calva, but a steady diet of it would be too sad, and wouldn't be great for my liver, either.

– 9 –

The Revolution:
The Land Robert Parker
Forgot to Review

The Loire was the first wine region I ever traveled to, and ironically enough it was with my first love, Mr. Straight Laced.
Clutching a spray of purple freesias, he greeted me at Charles de
Gaulle. From there, we took our bicycles, headed to the train station, and got off the train in the town of Blois to start our journey. It was June 1981, and the hills around Vouvray were torture
for me. Mr. Straight Laced sweetly helped me up the inclines,
biking next to me, hand pressed to my back, pushing me up. He
tolerated my stopping at every limestone cave to taste wine and
at every sign that had a goat on it so I could sample the cheese.
At dinner, he couldn't drink. He tried, but I could tell he just had
no real feeling for it, and so I let him off the hook and relegated
myself to the *pichet,* whatever the restaurant happened to have on
hand. It was very sad. But here we are: Mr. Straight Laced is gone,
and the Loire is still with me.

The region starts two hours south of Paris and then hooks west, where it begins its sprawl toward the Atlantic. France's third-largest wine area, it produces the wine you're most likely to encounter in Paris.

If the world ever took the wines of Loire seriously—Who knows? When people get tired of the big fruity, oaky wines of the world, they might—all would agree that the region is home to benchmark Sauvignon and Chenin Blanc, not, as some think, New Zealand. If people cared about the grape of Muscadet, Melon de Bourgogne, they would obviously think the Nantais is its home region. And if anyone cared at all about the grape, they would know that this is the regal home of Cabernet Franc. Then there are what Mr. Rovani would have called those *talking dogs,* the violetty Côt, the peppery Pineau d'Aunis, and the fabulous local Grolleau and Gamay. These grapes are royals, like the more robust Cabernet Sauvignon, Merlot, Pinot, and Chardonnay. But the world does not live by foie gras alone; sometimes, the perfect potato or an apricot can be the most delicious flavor.

These wines have held the attention of anyone I've ever poured them for. Côt has a special place in my history. It isn't merely the wine I reach for when returning from California, in need of an antidote to that state's overblown fruit bombs. A wine with magical powers, it was the first to show the Owl Man grace. It was the wine he often prostrated himself in front of, the wine that showed him the milk of human kindness. Yes, that wine softened his soul.

Once or twice a year, Big Joe takes a motley crew of sommeliers, wine directors, and wine buyers on a Loire trip to visit the vignerons, thus establishing strong bonds and obligations—not to mention that it's easier to sell a wine with a story. By the time the buyers return home, they have plenty of tales to tell. The first time I dovetailed my own trips to coincide with Joe's was for the *New York Times*. I was to trail this group of passionate wine geeks who adored my kind of "talking dogs." Luckily for me (or for the *Times,* which was paying my tab), Joe picked cheap hotels. Some of them were so spooky that I had to counter the scary nights with extravagant linen sheets, whirlpool baths, room service, and wi-fi fantasies. On the first night, I was stashed away at the two-star Grand Hotel Saint-Aignan, not far from Clos Roche Blanche. It was run by a starched-white-collared, dispirited woman who resembled Agnes Moorhead in an ax-murderer film. But I was jet-lagged and I told myself it didn't matter—after all, I had walked the winter vineyard of the old Côt vines and saw the yellow rocks sticking out of the soil like old knee bones.

Something that really bolstered me was an exquisite evening spent at Pierre and Catherine Breton's winery. The feisty Bretons—both trained winemakers—are darlings of the Loire wine world, with a marriage reviewed as often as their wines. While Jacqueline Friedrich's 1996 book *Wine & Food Guide to the Loire* described the emerging winemaker Pierre as "every bit of a yuppie" and I have seen him behave like a frat boy, carrying women on his shoulders in the frenzies after wine-tasting bacchanals, he and his wife are true vignerons, dedicated to biodynamics and natural wines, and they make beautiful wines. Can they help it if they clean up well? But that night, his manner at a candlelit dinner in the winery was more subdued. He showed tremendous generosity by pouring us a 1947 Breton Clos Senechal made by his grandfather. This Cabernet (Franc, but in the Loire you assume Franc and not Sauvignon) was a pale plum color that burst out, with a really pretty aroma of ghostly bread and cherry pie underneath the first whiff and a taste of allspice and clove. After tasting it I thought of something my mother has taken to repeating: Old people all look alike. I'm beginning to see what she means, at least from a distance—a little bent, white hair, eyes dancing. Old wines, whether Pinot, Cab Franc, or Syrah, develop aromas and flavors like the ones that came from the spice box my grandfather used to pass around on Saturday night as part of the ritual prayer for ending the Sabbath and the beginning of the new week: the muted smells of allspice, clove, and cinnamon. The spices change from wine to wine, but they all summon up the spice box. And because I am who I am, I like old people and old wine.

I managed to get through to morning in my eerie hotel, but woke with the kind of misery known to hikers who have been caught in a bitter rain. I thought I'd go and get some breakfast, but after taking a look at the Ted Kaczynski–like owner, all snaggle-toothed and scruffy, I decided to find a nice salon de thé, where I had the best, most buttery financier ever. Yes, this is the life of a pampered wine journalist. All in a day's work.

The next stop after the Bretons' was Clos Rougeard in Saumur-Champigny. Big Joe and I walked from the supermarket parking lot to the domaine. He had been holding me at arm's length for the past few days while he dealt with his customers. He said, "Clos Rougeard is a cult estate. In France, every three-star restaurant hustles to get a small allocation. In America, outside of the few, no has heard of it." The Clos Rougeard's top wine sells on a wine list at about 150 dollars, the retail price of many Napa Cabernets, a bargain. Before the 2007 Schildknecht review the *Advocate* never wrote about it; Parker has scarcely covered Cabernet Franc in the three decades he has been reviewing wines. In fact, he is known for reviling the grape. That schlump Miles in the film *Sideways* reviled the grape as well. Wonder where he got that from?

We walked down to Rougeard's ancient cellars, where thousands of bottles were painstakingly stacked and accumulating a dense, furry crust, like you see on well-aged *saucission*. It was there, as the cellar cold refrigeratored me, that I realized how strange it was that no one in the Loire had invoked the Parker name. When I asked why, Nadi Foucault, one of the two brothers who own and work the winery, said, "Mr. Parker doesn't like the taste of Cabernet Franc. And he doesn't come to visit. So why bother caring what he thinks?"

Nadi poured a brackish-looking wine into our glasses. We tried to guess its age. He revealed it to be a 1934 Cabernet Franc made by his grandfather. Then, with absolutely no irony, he said, "I have nothing against Mr. Parker. He seems like a lovely man. But I think he just doesn't have a curious palate. It might be as simple as that."

That was when it hit me that Parker's history of ignoring the Loire had been its salvation. Because Parker dismissed the red wines of the area, the Loire vineyards remained relatively cheap. It remains to be seen whether the *Advocate*'s new appreciation for Loire reds will have any effect on the region or the wines' mass appeal. Meanwhile, young winemakers can still afford to rent vines and set up shop. Many of them are unschooled, yet well tutored. Much of the new crop of wine artists in the Loire embrace natural wine making, shun any sort of cosmetic technology or toasted barrels, and work their land organically. Some have jumped on the biodynamic bandwagon. Quite a few struggle to make wine with no sulfur. What has emerged there is one of the happiest, tightest, party-happy, *terroir*-driven communities of natural winemakers in the world. It makes me think of this line from Dostoevsky's *Notes from Underground:* "The long and short of it, gentlemen, that it is better to do nothing! Better conscious inertia. And so, hurrah for the underground."

THE SKINNY FOOD WRITER had not yet seen my anti-Parker Loire. She'd been exposed to lovely, Zingy red tea–like Pineau d'Aunis. She'd sipped brilliant, foot-stomped Cab Franc. She'd drunk the Clos Roche Blanche wines as well, but she hadn't experienced the wild and wacky spirit of the anti-establishment wine area, nor the intense tasting referred to as the Dive Bouteilles, the fringe event that often took place the weekend before the Loire wine fair, the Salon des Vins de Loire, and one of the Nicolas Joly's Renaissance des Appelations.

The Dive's wines extend beyond the Loire; the host Loire wine-makers invite like-minded wine-making friends from other appellations and sometimes other countries. The first time I attended, no one talked to me. The second time, when it was held in limestone caves, I froze my ass off. Still, no one talked to me. I had to fight my way to a table to be poured a taste; winemakers pretended I was invisible. That said, unfriendly or not, if more men looked like these men at wine tastings in the States, more women would take good wine seriously and lay off the cutesy animal labels. And the wines? They were likewise wildly unusual, most still fermenting away months after the harvest. Vins naturel all.

Skinny was mulling over the pros and cons of tagging along this time.

"If you come," I said, dangling another carrot, "we'll have lunch with Nicolas at the Coulée de Serrant." She bought her ticket.

Nicolas wholly enjoys being Nicolas, and who wouldn't? In his sixties, he still has most of his charmingly disheveled (gray) hair; he is part poet, part professor, and part philosopher. His daughter Virginie works alongside him at Coulée. He has a gorgeous, age-appropriate wife who bakes bread. They live in the mystical winery and vineyards at Coulée de Serrant, in Savennières, overlooking the Loire River, where winemaking has been documented as far back as the early twelfth century. And Nicolas is the unofficial leader of the worldwide biodynamic wine movement, taking the tastings known as Renaissance des Appelations, the Return to Terroir, around the world.

Biodynamics is a holistic way of farming tied to the seasons, the moon, and the planets. Elements in the vineyard are broken down to heat, air, water, and stone. Despite a lot of vinous psychobabble surrounding biodynamics, the movement offers much wisdom. This agrarian philosophy stems from a series of lectures delivered in 1924 by Rudolph Steiner called "Spiritual Foundations for the Renewal of Agriculture," which drew on the wisdom of the ancients, who had nothing to guide them but observation. Though biodynamics is indeed organic farming, there are big differences in approach and practice. Both models eschew the use of artificial fertilizers and synthetic chemicals. But organic is a reactive approach to the challenges of nature. Biodynamics is proactive, with a focus on building the health of the vineyard. Scheduling is proscribed; whether it's pruning your vines, treating the soil, or bottling the wine, practices are tied to the movement of the seasons, the planets, and the moon and influenced by careful observation of the four elements: earth, water, fire, and air. The concept of balance is key. Soil treatments focus on creating balance, to help the vines bolster themselves against parasites and insects. The concept of transformation is also essential—any treatment applied must itself have undergone some sort of transformation (such as fermentation, as in compost) or changed through dynamism (for example, stirred so vigorously that a vortex is created). The materials used for treatments are often animal (dung), mineral (quartz), or vegetal (herb). To deter what they see as the great environmental risk posed by a vinous monoculture, biodynamists work living farms, with horses, cows, and chickens—which provide the animal matter needed for treatments.

So what does all this make biodynamics? Perhaps it is a spiritual sort of organic farming that incorporates principles of Chinese medicine and the lunar calendar. Certainly, there is no end of fun to poke at the movement's disciples, but as more stunning wines emerge from their wineries, perceptions are changing. No matter what one thinks of this "religion," its principles demand an intensely intimate relationship between farmer and land, and how can that help but make a more vibrant wine?

Nicolas says the first time he attended a lecture on biodynamics, in 1978, he walked out, because it sounded like such hocus-pocus. But when he tasted the difference in wines produced biodynamically, he started to shift his ideology. And when he saw the difference in the soil of his vineyard—filled now with all sorts of life and fresh new smells, he was completely won over. He began to study, and went on to become a veritable Talmudist of the biodynamics movement. Some people believe that Joly and his biodynamics are voodoo, but others swear by them. In any case, many growers who follow the teachings are making terrific wine.

Nicolas's town, Savennières, is most famous for dry, long-lived, steely whites from the Chenin Blanc grape. Skinny and I drove into what looked like a Cotswold village, with its narrow lanes lined by walls and hedges. The lane leading to his estate was surrounded by vineyards, pasture, horses, sheep, fowl, and cows. There were several buildings on the property. A young woman bundled in woolens with dark, wild hair and rough hands met us and ushered us into a library cluttered with books, pipes, paintings, and photographs. She didn't introduce herself. It was only the next day, at the Angers tasting, that I realized she was Nicolas's daughter Virginie. She is ready to take over the mantle, very much like Maria José in Rioja and Maria Teresa in Barolo.

Nicolas floated in as if suspended on strings. He wore a sky-blue cashmere turtleneck, red-and-green plaid scarf, and beige wide-wale cords. He looked like the Fool in the Tarot deck, one of my favorites. The Fool is a happy man. His breastbone pointed to the sky, he basks in the sun while carrying a tiny hobo sack of sorrows on his shoulder. And he's about to step off a cliff. The Fool is a symbol of optimistic and healthy denial. I have no doubt that when the Fool falls, his sack turns into a parachute.

I had been told not to worry about the interview, all I needed to do was say hello and sit down, and Nicolas would proceed to talk. I introduced Skinny and myself. In the midst of stacked-paper chaos, we sat ourselves on the plump, chintz-covered couch and he asked to the air, "Where to start?" He didn't wait for an answer before he began chattering about biodynamics, his Return to Terroir tasting series, and the current crisis in the wine world.

Nicolas has a full vocabulary of body language. Operating with total integration of the vertical, horizontal, and sagittal planes, he uses a range of movement and all dimensions—a sign of someone who embraces life. He hugs, slashes, reaches, taps himself, stomps, punches, and floats. When he talks, his body dances. What does all this mean? Well, he may be a little nuts, but any visionary is.

His movement repertoire is as balanced and organic as the biodynamics he preaches. Nicolas says that it is important to observe the surroundings for clues to the health of a grape vine. If the leaves droop to the ground, look at the weeping willow tree to judge if the soil holds too much water. If the vine's leaves are dry, look at the cyprus, a tree of the sun that reaches up to the sky. Nicolas also observes the distinct nature of the manure produced by different animals. For example, some animals are dominated by heat, as are horses. Forced to move, cows will kneel down; biodynamists see these animals as ruled by an earth force. Wild boar and pigs feed on roots, so their manure will work on the roots of the vines. Each manure is essential in a different treatment. I found my host's use of observation to resonate with my training in the observation of movement as a dance therapist: A person keeping elbows pinched in close to the body may be avoiding moving forward in life, or a person may regulate the depth of the breathing essentially to protect the heart and emotions.

In all, we had two hours of conversation. Or perhaps more of a lecture, filled with wonderful Nicolisms, such as

The more people want fast food, the more there is room for slow.

Many parts of California shouldn't grow wines.

The new biodynamic enthusiast is like a young dog hunting
on the first day. This new generation is fabulous. They were
made for this biodynamics.

People say, "Show me the science of biodynamics." Look, as a
farmer you need water. How does it help you to know that
water is H_2O?

All of this would irritate my friend Roger Boulton at UC
Davis, but Nicolas spoke with as much conviction as Aubert de
Villaine of Domaine Romanée Conti did when he'd said, "You
can deny God, if you wish, but not that the sun rises."

Finally Nicolas looked at his watch and said, "My wife will be
angry with us. We must go to lunch." It was then I realized that
the petite chateau we were in was not his house, but his office.
His house was a few meters down the hill, in an old monastery,
which looked more like a *Wuthering Heights* crofter's cottage. His
wife was a visual match for him, tall with long bones, long, silky
hair, and a natural beauty. I was amused that bottles of supple-
ments were clustered on the table and that the Jolys considered
ham-infused carrot salad suitable for non–meat eaters. I smelled
the ham before any of it found its way into my mouth, and trying to be discreet, switched my attention to the potatoes. I am
crazy about a good potato. Those tender potatoes, *rattes*—yup,
my answer to foie gras. The pike-perch was perfectly poached,
meaty and sweet with a tangy and lemony butter sauce, and Mme.
Joly's rye bread was tart and warm.

During the meal we were served some of Nicolas's Savennières.
I spied on him to see if he had any to drink. There was some in

his glass, but did he raise it to his lips? I was snoopy because several people in the wine business had told me that he didn't drink. So I decided to ask him straight out. "Do I drink wine? Yes, of course," he answered. "I hate to drink too much, and am not at ease around people who are overdrinking! The first person to write that I hate wine was a woman journalist from the United States about twenty years ago. She was never interested in hearing anything about true wines and only interested in things like the name of my grandmother."

I was relieved. It was one thing for Steiner to abstain—he wasn't a winemaker.

Later, curled up by the fire, Skinny and I sat ready to resume listening. It is so easy to fall into disciple mode. I felt as if we were young revolutionaries hiding in the forest, absorbing rhetoric while Nicolas gesticulated, sucked on his pipe, and told stories. Steiner books were stacked everywhere; Nicolas read them daily. In starting his Renaissance group, Nicolas's aim was to slowly create consumer awareness about authentic wines, not only biodynamic wines but also all those that represent *terroir*. "You see," he said, "the wine consumer has no idea. They have no idea. They like artificial flavor. Look, at the Renaissance tent in Bordeaux, we did a tasting of real versus commercial. We first offered carrots, and then milk. Everyone loved the flavor of real carrots against the ones from the *supermarché*. That was easy. But there were people who liked the taste of long-life milk better than fresh milk."

"Actually," Skinny said, "is that such a problem?"

He didn't understand. So she continued. "Not everyone has to like the real thing. There are limited resources for natural wine; there is not a whole lot of it around. More for the people who care about it?"

"I suppose that's one way of looking at it," he said, taking a drag from that Sherlock Holmes pipe of his.

I said, "There are some people who prefer instant coffee to real stuff. Some people prefer polyester to silk. It's what they are used to. If they have the right palate and aesthetic, and are exposed to something authentic, they will understand. Here's the real problem. When the long-life milk claims it is real milk, that's the problem. You see?" I was remembering that wonderful conversation with Baldo Cappellano in Piedmont. "The problem is that 'technical' wines are taken as real."

And then the conversation came around to the certain critics who don't help the situation. As he petted his aptly named dog, La Lune, Nicolas said, "I was in Burgundy at Domaine Jadot, having lunch with Jacques Lardier [the esteemed Jadot winemaker] and Anne-Claude Leflaive [of her own domaine], both of whom practice biodynamics. Pierre Antoine Rovani was there, too. During the lunch I said to Rovani, 'Don't you think it's time to look at the technology and its effect on the wine world?'

"And he said, 'why, if it makes good wine, is there a problem?'

"Anne Claude said to me, 'why do you try, Nicolas? You know he doesn't get it.'"

Before we left, we visited the Coulée, the hill of vines overlooking the river. Then we went to see the cows that provided the dung for fertilizing and the chickens that pecked the bugs from the vineyards and provided the egg whites for fining impurities from the wine. It was all so picturesque, I thought, a media dream. I said to Nicolas, "People are worried that biodynamics will be used as a marketing tool. I used to think it was so work-intensive that it was safe, but now I see there is a risk. Do you?"

"Yes," he said. "When some fool claims they are biodynamic because they look at the moon, that is the real danger. Yes, people will use it. This is always a risk."

Jenny Lefcourt, a Paris-based American wine importer of mostly hardcore natural wines, told me about visiting wine stores in New York City with Bernard Belahsen, a winemaker from Languedoc who brought pictures of his horse working the field, as many biodynamists prefer. One shopkeeper, a Frenchman who had been a sommelier at a high-profile New York restaurant, said to him, "I am so sick of these people with their pictures of their horses," inferring that this was a marketing technique. An offended Jenny told the shopkeeper that her vigneron, whose label is Fonte-dicto, had worked with a horse for fifteen years, long before using horses became a status symbol. In fact, many of the most passion-ate followers of biodynamics keep their practices quiet. Many don't even apply for the certification of Biodivin or Demeter. In our advertising-driven world, authenticity is something a hired-gun marketing expert can manufacture. I shudder at the thought of wineries implying the use of biodynamics by showing pictures of the moon in advertising. It will happen, if it isn't already—pretty ads showing a full moon and some ram's horns! I used to think that biodynamics was too much work, that it would never go mainstream. I suppose I used to feel the same way about organic winemaking. Once organics became big business, however, the concept got watered down. For example, in the United States, consumers can easily pick up a wine labeled *Made with organic grapes,* but what's in the bottle could well be laden with chemicals and additives. By now, to be labeled organic, only 70 percent of a product has to meet organic standards. Take free-range chickens. Just because the chicks run free doesn't mean they are fed organically—yet this is implied. Just because the milk is organic at Whole Foods Market doesn't mean that the cows are treated humanely. The letter of the law is met but the spirit is lost. When this happens with biodynamics, I'll have another battle to fight.

When we left Nicolas that day, he said good-bye the same way he signs his e-mails. "Keep going!" he said.

THE MEDIEVAL TOWN of Angers is close to chateaux country. In the summer the region is lush and imposing fairy-tale castles peep out of the trees like jewels in Harry Winston windows. But in February a certain gray clings to France, especially to this deeply, darkly medieval town, where the looming fortress takes on an imposing, nearly sinister look.

When we arrived at Chateau Angers where the Dive Bouteilles tasting was being held the scene I had promised Skinny was in full force.

We could already feel the boisterous energy of tasters as we walked toward the dungeon where the action was. On the way I bumped into Aubert, who reiterated his offer to have me come pick at harvest time in Burgundy. Then he hurried away to give his talk. As we continued down to the entrance of the Dive, we passed a sign forbidding neckties.

Once inside, I saw many Parisian wine-bar owners I recognized who stared at me, trying to place this familiar-looking, short, red-haired woman. In my peripheral vision, I caught a glimpse of Big Joe and his following. This was the first year I was not his tagalong. I was on my own with Skinny. And something else was different.

In any social world, unless you're extremely beautiful or famous, you have to pay your dues. Sometimes this means showing up enough to finally become a familiar face. For two years, I had to fight for a place at the Dive's tasting tables. Now crowds parted for me. Vignerons addressed me with, "Ça va?" Winemakers showing off their wines immediately spoke to me. Now they mostly understood my French instead of pretending not to. They poured their wines, asked for my opinion.

Skinny was very impressed with the view. "Every hipster in Paris is here. I've never seen this many good-looking men in one room in my life, and they all know you!"

The Dive has a high percentage of winemakers who are into the no-sulfur thing. Some are more successful than others. These kinds of wines are considered the ultranatural of the naturals and are currently the darlings of the explosive Paris and Tokyo natural wine scenes. I appreciate these wines and I appreciate the desire for little intervention, and I would rather drink these wines than anything that's been plopped in toasty oak, but they can have a disturbing sameness. I often find their weight and aromatics similar. In blind tastings I can get confused about the grape varietal. Sometimes the wines feel a little unfinished to me, with an aftertaste I call puppy breath. Other no-sulfur wines are simply exciting. At a tasting in Paris once, a friend of mine who loves wine had her first experience with a bunch of them. "I see," she said. "These are what wines used to taste like. It's something that we're just not used to anymore." And then I knew what Francesco had meant when he said something similar about the Dard et Ribo wines.

Wines made without sulfur often need tender care, such as careful, cool shipping and cool storage. Many adore decantation. I often dump them into a big-mouthed, open pitcher, and in a few hours they can redefine themselves again and again. There were once wonderful bargains in the category, though the fall of the dollar over the past few years has had an impact. They still, however, give great value as against most of the overpriced domestic wines. One thing is for sure, for better or worse—and mostly for the better—the wines have vitality. Big Joe has a few of these ultranaturals, but many of these "extreme" winemakers' wines are becoming available in the States thanks to Jenny Lefcourt, who moved from Brooklyn to Paris to finish her Ph.D. in French film. She fell in love with a French piano player and winemaker, Francois Ecot, and they became Jenny & Francois, wine importers. The Jenny & Francois romance has progressed into business and friendship. They prefer their wines to have no added sulfur at all.

Jenny swung an invitation for us to the Dive's after party in a medieval theme park of a restaurant in downtown Angers. Veritable walking Robin Hoods and Joans of Arc, staff and musicians, all in period leggings and robes, banged ouds and bowed gambas and doubled as servers. We were all encouraged to put on costumes ourselves. Skinny and I declined. Unlike uptight Americans, though, the winemakers seemed to get into the spirit with an infectious innocence. Over the next hours the staff played and sang loudly and wildly, working the group into a frenzy. A mad, carousing line of winemakers and god knows who else dragged Skinny and me down the stairs in a circle dance that snaked through the huge building. Pierre Breton, true to reputation, hoisted some *femme* onto his shoulders. Shaggy Olivier Cousin danced wildly with his wife. I was being whipped around, faster and faster. When it all got too out of control and I feared my arm would be ripped from its socket, I slipped out of the chain as if running across the border. I took a moment to relish my escape only to look back and see poor Skinny in the middle of the circle like a virgin sacrifice. Her enthusiastic tormentor was Jean-Pierre Robinot, of l'Ange Vin winery. Robinot is a beloved figure to many young vignerons. Before he turned winemaker, he was one of its early promoters at his Paris wine bar twenty years ago.

A wiry man, he has always reminded me of Rumpelstiltskin. I saw the look with which he devoured poor Skinny. I would have been terrified if I were in her boots, but I couldn't help but watch with a little bit of mirth. When she shot me a *Save me!* look I figured I had to help. I took one more second than I should have.

Then I could see Robinot's sweat dripping all over her. At last I cut in and spirited her back to the table for safety. I've been to crazy gatherings before, but nothing mixed such mirth with wine. This scene was the fountain of youth, and Robinot was the proof of it.

It was a bit ironic: How could they keep me down in Paris after I'd seen the farm? After experiencing such lively times at the alternative tastings, how could the dull Salon de Loire have a chance with me? At the Salon the T-shirts and tattoos of the day before were traded in for button-down shirts and sportscoats. But much worse than the formality were most of the wines. Just as at the fringe Italian tasting, most of the Dive wines were meritorious—and at the conventional Salon there was no relief. While I can point to maybe forty regional producers who make exquisite wine, there are plenty of truly bad wines made in the Loire. There are many passionless winemakers who overcrop, machine harvest, farm with chemicals, and use lab-made yeast. Unfortunately, most of the 740 million gallons of wine produced in the area sucks.

I ended up taking refuge at the Clos Roche Blanche booth, where Big Joe was tasting with his crew. He was in the middle of telling the story about how he found CRB with David Lillie (now owner of Chambers Wine and Spirits and such a supporter of Loire wines that I think of him as Mr. Loire). Mr. Loire had fallen in love with the wines back in his saxophone playing days. He fell for these wines because of their extreme character, and it didn't hurt that they delivered a terrific pop for the buck. Once Mr. Loire had segued into the wine retail biz, he and Joe started to scout the Salon together. This time they were trawling for wines from Touraine, the center cut of the region. There were lots of dreadful wines from the area at that time, when the wine consultants came telling winemakers they had to machine harvest and yeast and otherwise treat their wines. "God only knows how many we tasted," Big Joe said. "Between the high level of sulfur and the uniform sameness of all these wines, I was getting worn out. So I approached one of the last Touraine tables and asked the smiling owner if they harvested by machine and used inoculated yeasts. When she said yes, I thanked her and told her we would not be interested."

The next morning, he and Mr. Loire were eating breakfast at their hotel and the same woman Big Joe had arrogantly dismissed came by. Once again, she was all smiles. She told them of her close friend who was making exactly the type of wine they were looking for. Could they rush to the exposition hall? Her friend would be there first thing, ready to receive them. So they rushed. They waited. They felt like chumps. Catherine and Didier arrived thirty minutes late. Not in the best of moods by now, Big Joe and his friend tasted the wines, which had honesty and precise flavors. Mr. Loire ordered a crazy amount of wine. And thus a cult winery for wine geeks with limited resources was born.

IT WAS JUNE when I next returned to the Loire. I took the train from Paris to the chateau town of Blois, where I picked up my rental car. The day was clear and squeaky clean. It looked exactly as I remembered it from twenty-five years earlier, when I started out from the town on a bike trip. Everything seemed to be in slow motion, washed in a creamy light. A gaggle of cabbies gathered underneath the shade of what looked like a mimosa tree. As I approached, one warty cab guy reached up among the fernlike leaves, pulled out two cherries, and offered them to me. They looked exactly like some plastic cherry earrings that Honey-Sugar had. I noticed the moment. I didn't mark the moment with fear, but I noticed it.

An hour later, I was driving in my cute metallic-green Fiat alongside of the Cher River. Thirsty, I remembered the fruit and popped one cherry into my mouth. Then I popped the other. They were neither sweet nor bitter, but they were wet. In a few minutes I started to get a headache. By the time I took the left up the road to Clos Roche Blanche, I had significant body ache. But there was no time to be sick, I thought, as I caught my first glimpse of the house, perched up on a hill. This house is built right on top of the wine cave. It is made of the local limestone—tuffeaux. There are vines sculpted into the foundation, and it reminds me in some ways of a lighthouse, a beacon of truth. Catherine's great-grandfather built the house. He was a wealthy man in textiles who lived only a few kilometers away, in town, but liked to take his Sunday lunch in the dining room, whose windows looked out at scenery for miles around. I suspect he may have engaged in less pure activities as well, but anyway, it was this great-grandfather who decided to put in vines, simply because he thought it would be nice to have some plants around.

Catherine moved back to this odd and beautiful house in 1975, when her father died, too young at age fifty-one. She didn't even like wine then; her motivation was a love for the house and the land. Because she and Didier Barrouillet had mutual friends, he came to work the harvest in 1981. But Catherine, who had had enough after six years of cooking for the twenty or so grape pickers, decided to replace the pickers with a machine. The man who, until then, was making the wine had to drive the tractor. So Didier, who knew nothing about making wine, shared the winemaking duties with Catherine. It was their first vintage. Catherine hated the process of making wine. "I am not patient," she said, "and to be a winemaker you need patience." But Didier was built for patience. She asked him to stay on for room and board, and he never left. It's hard to imagine them anywhere else. In a few years they realized that machine picking was inferior, and they went back to picking grapes by hand.

To get to the vineyards, I walked up a wooded country path that cuts the forest where Catherine hunts for mushrooms. The top of the road opened up to fields of vines. The Côt vines have been there for 110 years, since Catherine's great-grandfather had the wisdom to plant them. Pleasing as it was to see them in the late spring, I think I found the vineyard even more beautiful in the winter, with their gnarled vines seeming to grasp for warmth and the bonelike stones in the earth more visible. Now, in the middle of the Côt, I began to feel concerned. I was nauseous. I began to wonder, paranoically: Poisoned cherry?

I made it to dinner without embarrassing myself in the vineyards, or letting on how sick I felt. Catherine's daughter, a tall,
gorgeous girl who had just given her hair a buzz cut, made a vegetable crumble, in honor of me. There was salad, local cheese,
and good bread from a local baker who only uses wild yeast. Didier joined us. He's got such a fascinatingly angular face, much like
an animated Antonello da Messina portrait, with sucked-in cheeks
and screws of black hair. He laid out all of his wines from the
2005 vintage, helping to give me an appetite for food. Didier told
some of his story; to make up for his lack of wine schooling, he
had hired an adviser.

"Back in the eighties," he said, "you never questioned your
enologue. Mine told me to use yeast, and I used yeast. The enologue would always have me add the maximum amount of sulfur. And of course, enzyme. One year I used that Beaujolais yeast
in my Sauvignon Blanc, and it tasted and smelled like bananas."

What changed his course in winemaking was a conversation
with Noël Pinguet—the son-in-law of Vouvray's most famous
wine producer of Chenin Blanc, Gaston Huet. Pinguet believed
in making a wine naturally, no yeasts, enzymes, inoculation, or
anything that would make a wine speak more of technique than
of nature. Didier began to change in his thinking. By the time Big
Joe and Mr. Loire Lillie found Didier and Catherine at the Salon
de Loire, and by the time I tasted that Côt for the first time, they
were part of the small but growing Loire community of natural
wine people, and had a following in Paris.

Catherine and I spent quality time with the Gamay, extolling its virtues with each sip. While I do adore the Côt, a wine that is next to godliness, I often say, "*Toujours* Gamay." I can drink it every night, easy. It's complex, interesting, foodworthy. What's not to love? The CRB Gamay has been another of the Dressner cult wines. In fact, it is famous for a funkiness that some have likened to pondscum but in time deepens into crushed roses. And of course, the more we drank, the looser we got. The name Parker came up. The daughter, bless her heart, didn't know who he was. "He is the most powerful wine critic in the world," Catherine told her. "Even more powerful than Michel Bettane." Ah, yes, she remembered.

When I asked Didier what he thought of Parker he said, "I don't like churches." Which is also why he doesn't religiously follow biodynamics.

Toward the end of the night, I brought up my observation that the wealthiest people don't make the best wines. Didier found this quite funny, and agreed. Catherine was visibly uncomfortable, and she fidgeted. "I am making more money now," she said apologetically.

"Catherine," I said, "I know that you are the woman who has everything, but you have a computer filled with viruses that's ten years old, you are trying to replace your tuna tin of a car. You are rich because you can buy organic bread and the best cheese in the world, and you have this land that you love. But wealthy? You're making a living. You're entitled." I went on. "Look, this year the director of Chateau Lagrezette, a large domaine in Cahors, came over to dinner. The famous wine consultant Michel Rolland makes wine for the owner. I thought it would be fun for my friend to taste your Côt, which of course is the same grape used in Cahors Malbec. My friend was stunned. He looked at the wine, then at me. 'Who makes this wine?' he said, filled with appreciation. He said, 'This is what I've been saying: It takes a lot of money to make a wine like this.'

" 'Jean, I paid fifteen dollars for that wine,' I told him. He was stunned. Chateau Lagrezette starts at thirty dollars and goes up to 160.

"The rich hire Michel Rolland because they can afford to. They buy technology because they can afford to. They buy land in trendy areas because they can afford to. They buy bottles that weigh as much as wine because they can afford to. They buy status because they can afford to. Their world is all about wearing a label, the way people line up to buy vinyl-impregnated Louis Vuitton. You can buy a wine's body; however, you cannot buy its soul."

Having blown my energy on that speech, I went off to bed sooner than I would have liked. Sick again? I couldn't believe it. It seemed as if every time I'd traveled in the last few years, I succumbed. If I was writing a screenplay, I suppose I could use this as a plot twist. I was being poisoned by the globalists!

I packed myself under as many blankets as I could. The nighttime temperature had fallen, but even so I was unnaturally chilled. That damned taxi driver! I lay in bed shaking so hard that I thought I'd break bones. When I finally fell asleep, I dreamed of having a wild fever. I also dreamed of Catherine's attachment to the land and her home. Didier knew exactly what he was saying when he swore that Catherine didn't have feet, she had roots.

Something happened on that Loire trip, other than my getting sick. The flight home was the first flight in two years where I didn't walk off the plane puffy eyed from heartbreak tears. While I was in France or in Italy or Spain I had been relatively free, but heading home always tore a new hole in my heart. When I walked into my apartment after hefting my suitcase up the creaky old tenement stairs, the cartons of wine had been moved inside and carefully stacked, milk was in the refrigerator and gorgeous lilies and orchids filled the vase on my kitchen table, courtesy of Mr. Bow Tie. Healing from heartbreak, falling in love, and ripening grapes all take time.

But grapes are a little more predictable. Grapes need one hundred days to ripen. I had started to count the days, because I fully intended to head back to France to pick grapes for the harvest. But then the summer weather, perhaps teased by an unpredictable effect of global warming, threw another kink into the works. July was beastly, with desert-hot conditions. Winemakers were thinking harvest would be in August, way sooner than one hundred days. Then August it was cold and rainy! By September first the weather was more sensible, but Burgundy—where I had hoped to pick—had moved its harvest date to late that month. I thought, No wonder there aren't Orthodox Jewish vignerons. Harvest doesn't take the High Holy Days into account. That wasn't going to work. I was brought up Orthodox, in a house where actions as simple as turning on a light or opening mail were forbidden on shabbos. Even though I now live in the secular world, there was no way I was going to pick grapes on the Day of Atonement.

I sent Catherine an e-mail: *When are you guys picking?*

It turned out that the weather was lovely, the grapes were ripening, and they would start on the eleventh.

I quickly sent her another e-mail: *Journalist in need of* vendange!

I didn't hear back for two days. *Oh no, those damn Americans who think working the harvest is fun,* I could hear her thinking. And then finally, an e-mail arrived.

Dear Alice

I am feeling like being to accept! You can come because it is the beginning of harvest and we are not too much busy . . . Don't forget your boots and raincoat (actually it is sunny but you know "the times they are changing" . . .) and old jeans, sweaters, because it is a dirty job!

P.S.: Take an alarm clock; you'll need it to get up on the morning!

Picking at Domaine Romanée Conti would have been a privilege, but being able to pick at CRB seemed to be divine intervention.

My desire to pick was met with concern. Mr. Bow Tie worried about my hands—I have all sorts of repetitive stress pains from typing, and besides, he knew I wasn't the sturdiest girl. A fashionable Parisian friend warned me to take knee pads because of all the kneeling. The Owl Man, who resurfaced from time to time to do my taxes and fix things like my pull-chain toilet, recommended gardening gloves to avoid blisters from working the *secateurs* for hours. My mother, knowing my lack of passion for hard physical labor, told me, "You know, you're nuts." You would have thought I'd told them I was going to climb Kilimanjaro. A few days before I left, though, I wondered if I *was* in my right mind. Some odd pain flared up in my left leg (Oh no! I am old. Is that what they call sciatica?), and my right hand started to scream from all of the typing it was doing. I was not in great shape.

To make everything worse, this was the first time I had flown since the new Draconian rules forbidding liquids on board. I had to drink scotch—bad scotch at that. The wine available on airlines is felonious. Once I was on French land, just before I stepped up to pay my fare, the Roissy bus ran over my luggage, missing my foot by centimeters.

With a suitcase that looked like a fallen soufflé, I picked up the rental car in Roissy and ended up at Catherine's house a mess. She, on the other hand, looked terrific. Her hair cut into a longish pageboy, she was fit, and grinning like a little kid. She embraced me, then showed me her hands flashing her palms in my face. They were stained raven black, and it was Sunday—they hadn't picked since Friday. "You see what your hands will look like?" she said, laughing. The harvest had taken ten years off of her. She was fired up with the excitement of the vintage. Hope. And excitement. A year's work coming to its climax.

Solange, Catherine's mother, arrived from Blois—home of the poisoned cherries—to take care of us. With silken, paper-white hair swept up in an elegant twist, lively, expressive eyes, and posture straight out of Catholic school, this widow twice around had no widow's hump. And what's more, she was a crack cook. She spoke no English, and was saintly about putting up with mine. The next few days were a love fest. She said, "I was afraid to meet an American. I thought they were all like George Bush, but now I see I was wrong."

At dinner the first night, I again thanked Catherine for letting me come, and promised her I wouldn't hold back on the work.

"We thought it would be so funny to see you in the vines," she said, and then laughed—not with me, but at me. I saw it then: I would be their own personal Jerry Lewis. Laugh she might, though, because I had my doubts that I would be able to stand up straight after the first day; I might never make it to the second or the third. I did not want her reporting to the people we both knew that I was useless. When I went to bed, I asked what time I was expected. She said, "Oh, Alice. Don't worry. Come and find us whenever you want."

That night my hands hurt. My sciatica hurt. You old bird, I thought, welcome to middle age. It was a good thing that I had a Mr. Bow Tie at home who blanketed me with compliments and thought I was beautiful. But in the wee hours, I had a screenplay of a dream, starring me and Skinny. We exited the car and were greeted by Catherine and a man with a chiseled face, sunken cheeks, and wiry hair, very much like Didier. He took one look at us and laughed in scorn. "Those women are going to work?" he cried. "Look how frail they are. And that one, the one with the red hair, she has no muscle!"

When I woke up, rain was streaming down. I was determined. Even if I landed in the hospital when I returned to America, I would pick until the death. Proud that I was just fifteen minutes late (picking starts at 8:00 AM), I headed out and up a path lined with wild cyclamen to the vineyards. I saw movement like white ducks swimming on top of the vines. As I got close I saw the workers kneeling at the vines, hands moving fast, and realized the ducks were three men with conical packs on their backs called *huttes*. The pickers each emptied his own little bucket of grapes into these larger *huttes,* which the *hutte*holders then emptied into a waiting truck. Catherine handed me clippers and a bucket and set me up on a row with a fast worker, who showed me how to cut away grape rot and select the healthy grapes.

The pickers were locals and a mixed group. There were a few retirees, like the housewife with the blue nitrol gloves who looked like she was about to scrub floors. There were some amorous students filled with randy energy and a few Gypsies, one who kept whistling "Oh Susanna," when I was near him.

In the morning we picked Sauvignon Blanc grapes. The rain made it more difficult, because the grapes absorbed the water and easily burst, like water balloons, in my hands. With the rain, you must take care to look for rot, avoid the bad grapes, and concentrate on the good. By the time the ten-o'clock break came around, I felt I was getting the hang of things. Oddly, my right hand felt remarkably strong, with none of the nerve weakness I had gotten so used to.

The two-hour break for lunch was welcome. The workers went home, and Solange pampered us. Didier and Catherine were happy with their braised shoulder of pig, while I had a tender-lentil salad and a pure vegetable soup. Even after a lunch with wine, I was happy to get back into the fields. I felt the urgency of picking pressing upon me. The sun shone as our band of merry grape pickers moved on to the red grape Gamay. Because of the rain, and a threat of mold ruining the grapes, Catherine constantly barked to watch out for the rot. *"Faîtes attention pour les pourries!"* she cried. She pored over all of the grapes, making sure only healthy grapes got picked. Gamay, which makes one of my favorite wines, has supertight spacing between its fruit. I felt my power to help in every bunch I picked. Every time I snipped a bunch, I cut out the rot thinking, Oh no, you're not getting into my Gamay. Yet I also began to think . . . A little bit of that rot? Just a little bit? That was the secret to the note of pondscum in the wine that made the Clos Roche Blanche Gamay one of the best on the wine shelves.

By the afternoon break, some pickers had developed a curiosity about the interloper . . . me. The big-bicepsed, garlicky whistler asked if I was of Irish descent. I short-handed the answer. "No. Russian." He must have approved, because after that he treated me like a little sister, helping me tip up my little bucket to the *hutte.* Another man, however, wasn't convinced about me. He yelled out, *"Êtes vous touriste?"* Then he asked how much I was paying Catherine. They were getting eight euros an hour—perhaps I was paying her double that?

The thought that someone would pay to pick was pretty funny. By the second half of the day, all of my muscles felt as if they had been put in a washing machine on spin. My hands were black and sticky from the juice. Everything was sticky, especially in the afternoon, when the heat baked the juice to my hair and clothes. The work was messy, tacky, and fragrant. It was as all-encompassing as when the Owl Man had me help him run new electrical wires in my apartment. In near one-hundred-degree heat, the plaster had fallen onto my head and in my hair and my eyes, and I was utterly miserable. I yelled at him, "Jewish girls weren't meant to do this kind of work!" But here, even though I was as sticky as a pot of glue, I was in gorgeous fields surrounded with sweet smells. I felt like a midwife assisting in the birth of wine. I was energized, not enervated. If the old beau could see me now, I thought. I now know what bunches of Sauvignon Blanc and Gamay feel like in my hand. This is no small thing. I have found out that grapes really don't have to be treated like pampered infants to create fantastic wine.

Just before sundown, after the picking and the carting of the grapes over to the winery, Catherine and I went back to the vineyards, this time to pick some of the *mousseline* mushrooms we had seen near the Gamay. There weren't many, just a few slender, flesh-colored fungi clustered in a ring, but we picked what we could and brought them back to make an omelette.

Catherine, an excellent hostess, wanted me to have the whole experience of fresh-picked mushrooms myself. Feeling the preciousness of the mushrooms, though, I insisted on splitting them with Solange, whose eyes lit up like an imp's. The omelette tasted better shared. I drank the Côt, the delicious, mineral wine, and went to bed.

The next morning, I woke ready to reach for the Motrin, but I was pain free. Frankly, I couldn't understand it at all, but just decided to accept that picking grapes was the world's best physical and emotional therapy. I was able to spend my next days clipping, lifting, squatting, bending, and springing, deerlike, among the vines. Catherine said that she was surprised, gave me a big hug, and told me she was going to tell Big Joe that I was a champ. She wasn't as surprised as I was. I continued to pick happily, convinced that this Clos Roche Blanche vintage would be one of the best.

– Acknowledgments –

Along the journey there were so many random (as well as pre-meditated) acts of kindness that helped in putting this book together. People put up with me (some even put me up), tolerated my questions and constant e-mails, supported me, edited me, taught me, and rooted for me.

Many thanks to Joe Dressner for taking that time in our initial meeting to open the doors of perception. Thanks to the crew at UC Davis, and particularly to Professor Roger Bolton for the dialogue.

I raise my hat to Thomas Perry in Rioja for insisting he drive and to the irrepressibly cute Maria José Lopez de Heredia for her generosity. Can I ever thank Francesco and Beatrice for nursing me back to health and taking me around and for twisting François Ribo's arm to see me? To my dear friend, Ronni Olitsky, so many adventures past and future. Thank you for your love and enthusiasm, for polishing my klutz when in Champagne.

I thank Moët Chandon for not taking out a hit on me and I thank the growers in that region for their bravery, working against the establishment and proving that one can grow without chemicals even in the area's dreadful weather! Many pitched in for the Italy adventure and my search for Scanavino. Jeremy Parzen changed my journata to giornata as well as e-mailed and persuaded. Thanks to Lars Leicht for his support, information, and for contributing the word *Scandalavino*! Ah, Elena Rovera, the fabulous visionary and friend from the Cascina del Cornale. *Baci.* And thanks to the Cerettos for letting Skinny and I stay at their bunker in the vines, and to cutie-pies Sam diPalo and his friend Daniele Mereu for interpreting with Marie Teresa Mascarello.

In Burgundy it is Russell and Becky and Becky and Russell. Love and thanks as always for so many meals and sheltering nights and talks and experiences and bottles. I could not have conceived this chapter without you. And to Clive, thanks for the cheeky quotes and letting me bug you while we tasted. I appreciate the help and time and poesy from distinguished Aubert de Villaine. I loved spending time with his refreshingly frank wife, Pamela. And to Philippe Pacalet for always opening up his cellar to me.

A great big thanks to Nicolas Joly for the long e-mails and the lovely lunch and just for being Nicolas. Keep going! To Stephanie Teuwen for her cheering on the sidelines and her work for the vignerons of the Loire. A toast to the winemakers of the Loire who have the guts to find a different path and luscious offerings to those who shun the points. And while I'm on the topic of the Loire, to Catherine and Didier for allowing me and Melissa to work the harvest as well as caring for us and making some of the wines that have changed my view of the world.

I do thank Robert M. Parker, Jr., for his time and contribution, and I really wasn't kidding when I said I hope to taste with him one day. I appreciate the wine importers like Louis/Dressner, Jenny & Francois, Jon David Headrick, Neal Rosenthal, Becky Wasserman, and Kermit Lynch and those I don't know about, for championing honest wines for the States and of course, because of them I can find many gorgeous wines to drink Stateside. May they be inspirational for all those winemakers who fret that they won't be able to sell their sensitive, expressive wines that just are.

Melissa Clark has been my travel buddy on so many occasions we've lost count. She was primarily instrumental in bolstering my confidence to get the book proposal done in the first place. After that fish-eye conference in Spain, when we discussed the sad state of Rioja, I mentioned this version of the book idea and she said, "That's it. That's the book you're going to write." She called it my destiny, and she kept encouraging, pushing, and coaching me and finally even I was convinced that I could put down the material in a way that would make the reader care. She traveled out of her own pocket, in friendship and support, often with no assignment to offset her cost. I am also very grateful she gamely shouldered the burden of being called Skinny for the book. Melissa, Slim just wouldn't have worked!

On the production side, thank God for friends. To Susan

Shapiro for pressing me to keep the Love present in this Battle. The super New York City caviste, David Lillie for his decades-long dedication to the wines of the Loire. Liz Reisberg, for pushing pencils at my fractured sentence structure and oddly placed commas and to my friend Stephen diRenza, who constantly read my raw copy whether he was in Paris or Fez and for letting me use his place in Paris, as if it were my own. To Ethel Feiring, who looks at me in shock, often not comprehending how I could be her daughter, but loves me nevertheless. To Alan Farnham for not only holding my hand through the writing but for finding me the best agents a girl could have, Betsy Amster and Bob Sehlinger, who in turn delivered me into the hands of Harcourt and my extremely brilliant editor Andrea Schulz who stunned me with her patience, Virgo-esque order, x-ray vision, and creativity. And thanks to my copyeditor, Marian Ryan. And, finally to RB, for fueling a lifetime of inspiration.

Index